Computing in Musicology

A Directory of Research

Center for Computer Assisted Research in the Humanities
Menlo Park, CA

Volume 7   **1991**

Editors:
>Walter B. Hewlett
>Eleanor Selfridge-Field

Assistant Editors:
>Meredith Berger
>Edmund Correia, Jr.

Advisory Board:
>Lelio Camilleri, Florence Conservatory
>John Walter Hill, University of Illinois
>John Howard, Harvard University
>Arvid Vollsnes, University of Oslo
>David Wessel, University of California at Berkeley

ISBN 0-936943-06-8
ISSN 1057-9478

Center for Computer Assisted Research in the Humanities
525 Middlefield Road, Suite 120
Menlo Park, CA 94025-3443
XB.L36@Stanford.Bitnet

Preface

Computing in Musicology started in 1985 as the *Directory of Computer-Assisted Research in Musicology*. As we complete our seventh publication in this series, we are impressed not only by the ever greater abundance of contributions but also by the broad range of perspectives brought to musical scholarship. To cope with this growing sophistication, we are presenting for the first time direct contributions in place of short summaries.

We have been challenged more than ever by both the quality and the complexity of the material submitted from fields outside musicology. This array of new areas of expertise brings into our midst distinct dangers of editorial misunderstanding or misinterpretation. The references that accompany many contributions will be helpful to those readers who, like ourselves, must master new vocabularies and look in unfamiliar places for documentation. Their appearance in this issue, however, is purely spontaneous, and the cacophony of editorial styles in contributing disciplines has forced us to adopt a style sheet for future years; it appears on the final page of this issue.

The reciprocal of an increasing volume of contributions is a diminishing amount of available space. We prefer to publish groups of articles on a related topic, and some valuable contributions that were received but not published this year may appear at another time. Our main emphasis remains on applications of value to those involved in musical scholarship and related professions. Prospective contributors should read the *Note* at the end of the book.

Although this is the longest issue we have published, it has often been necessary to summarize or eliminate discussion of procedure and technique, but a significant percentage of our contributors will cheerfully share their expertise, and sometimes their programs and their data, with interested readers. Each article provides information about how to contact the author. We receive many heartening letters concerning the value of *CM* as an intellectual match-maker.

We continue to be gratified by the prompt response of notation software developers to our annual packet of set pieces. They work very hard to submit purposely challenging material in a limited amount of time, and we greatly appreciate their efforts.

Neither the breadth nor the depth of this issue would have been possible without the dedicated effort of our staff members Frances Bennion, Meredith Berger, Edmund Correia, Jr., and Steven Rasmussen. Working in concert, they exhumed errors and inconsistencies at a pace far exceeding that of our automatic spelling and grammar checkers. We offer our special thanks to Clive Field and Michael McGuire for contributing their technical insights to the article on fractals. Finally, we welcome a roster of editorial advisers whose duties will begin in 1992. We hope you will give them the same support as you have given us.

October 9, 1991   *Menlo Park, CA*

Table of Contents

Current Chronicle

Appointments

North American Center for Machine-Readable Texts

The establishment of a North American Center for Machine-Readable Texts in the Humanities, explored in a symposium sponsored by Rutgers and Princeton Universities in March 1990, has come to fruition with the help of funding for general administration from the Mellon Foundation and for continuance of the preparation of an inventory of texts from the National Endowment for the Humanities. Susan Hockey of the Oxford Computing Service has agreed to serve as the Center's first director and is scheduled to assume her new duties in October 1991.

Books and Articles

CHUM Retrospective

"Computing in Musicology, 1966-91," a retrospective by Walter B. Hewlett and Eleanor Selfridge-Field, appears in the 25th anniversary issue of *Computers and the Humanities*, which is scheduled for publication in December 1991. *CHUM* is published six times a year by Kluwer Academic Publishers Group, PO Box 322, 3300 AH Dordrecht, The Netherlands.

The Computer and Epistemology

In examining the ways in which computers are being used in the humanities, and in particular in studying issues of knowledge representation in learned discourse, Jean-Claude Gardin has postulated the rise of a "third way of knowledge" in his collection of essays *Le Calcul et la raison: Essais sur la formalization du discours savant*, which is available from CID, 131 Boulevard Saint-Michel, 75005 Paris, France; tel. +34 43-54-47-15; fax 43-54-80-730.

Computers and Musical Style

David Cope's *Computers and Musical Style*, an exposition of the EMI [Experiments in Musical Intelligence] approach to simulation of individual styles of composition using procedures borrowed from artificial intelligence and significantly refined by the author, was scheduled for publication in October 1991 by A-R Editions (801 Deming Way,

Madison, WI 53717-1903) in the US and by Oxford University Press overseas. The hardcover publication carries the ISBN 0-89579-256-7.

The Computer in Musicology, Composition, and Pedagogy

Helmut Schaffrath is the editor of *Computer in der Musik: Ein Einsatz in Wissenschaft, Komposition und Pädagogik,* which was published in May 1991 [ISBN 3-476-30330-6] by J. B. Metzler Verlagsbuchhandlung in Stuttgart. Contributions on neural nets (Marc Leman), computer-assisted instruction (Bernd Enders), MIDI problems and possibilities (Christoph Micklish, Ulrich Bloman), algorithmic composition (Walter Schröder-Limmer, Dirk Reith), and analysis (Ioannis Zannos, Udo Will) follow a substantial introduction by the editor.

Computer-Aided Research in the Humanities

Art history, linguistics, and musicology are the chief areas explored in Christoph Schnell's *Ein System zur computergestützten Forschung in den Geisteswissenschaften: Konzeption, Implementierung, Anwendungsbeispiele* [ISBN 3-261-04197-8], published by Peter Lang in Bern in 1989. In particular this work describes the TIMES environment [*cf.* p. 159] for multi-faceted research on the Macintosh platform.

The *Electronic Musician* Guides

A brief description of the function of individual features and extensive tables indicating the particular features of many commercial programs for music processing have recently appeared in Dan Phillips' and Bob O'Donnell's "Guide to Sequencing Software" and in Christopher Yavelow's "Guide to Notation Software" in *Electronic Musician* 7/8 (1991), 38-50, and 9, 44-56 respectively.

IEEE Computer: Special Issue on Music Applications

"Computer-Generated Music" is the subject of the July 1991 issue of *IEEE Computer*. Denis Baggi served as guest editor of this issue. Traditional classical repertories are considered in David Cope's article on "recombinant" methods of simulating historical styles and Margaret Johnson's expert system for automatic articulation in Bach fugues. An article on Standard Music Description Language (pp. 76-9; see *CM 1990*, pp. 53-6) by Steven R. Newcomb is also of interest. The contact address is 10662 Los Vaqueros Circle, PO Box 3014, Los Alamitos, CA 90720-1264.

Informatics and Musicology

Lelio Camilleri's article "Informatica e musicologia: Codifica e catalogazione delle musiche antiche" appeared in *Musica antica* II (1990), 25-29. Brief reference to a number of projects, most familiar to readers of this publication, is provided.

Macintosh Music and Sound

Christopher Yavelow's *Macintosh Music and Sound Bible*, scheduled for publication in 1991, is an applications-oriented reference work emphasizing commercially available products and incorporating interviews with users. It will be available from IDG Books Worldwide, 155 Bovet Road, Ste. 730, San Mateo, CA 94402; tel. (415) 358-1258.

MTNA Guide to Software

The *MTNA Guide to Music Instruction Software*, published annually by the Music Teachers National Association, contains numerous evaluations of software for primary music education. The association's members are chiefly independent music teachers. The programs covered in the 1990 edition ($22 plus postage) were written between 1982 and 1988; each issue is cumulative. The guide is available from MTNA Publications, Ste. 1432, 617 Vine St., Cincinnati, OH 45202-2434.

Music Perception and Cognition

The *Proceedings of the First International Conference on Music Perception and Cognition*, held in Kyoto from October 17 to 19, 1989, are now available from the recently organized Society for Music Perception and Cognition. They may be obtained by writing to Manuel Gonzales, Society for Music Perception and Cognition, Dept. of Psychology, University of California at San Diego, La Jolla, CA 92093.

Music Processing

Goffredo Haus is the editor of the anthology *Music Processing*, which is scheduled for publication by A-R Editions in 1992. Articles on music description, music analysis, algorithmic composition, and computer music are included.

Musicus

Musicus: Computer Applications in Music Education, Volume 1 (1989), is reviewed by Stephen Page in the electronic *Music Research Digest* of February 3, 1991. *MRD* is available to network users in the United Kingdom from *archive-server@uk.ac.oxford.prg* and to those elsewhere from *archive-server@hplpm.hpl.hp.com*, as well as from *HUMBUL* [*cf.* p. 16]. The hardcopy publication *Musicus*, which includes many extensive user reports of software, is available within the UK for £10 and elsewhere for £15 per annum from the CTI Centre for Music, Department of Music, Lancaster University, Lancaster LA1 4YW, UK; e-mail: *L.Whistlecroft@lancaster.ac.uk*. *Musicus* is edited by Anthony Pople; Lisa Whistlecroft coordinates software information and subscriber services.

Musiknotation

Helen Wanske is the author of *Musiknotation: Von der Syntax des Notenstichs zum EDV-gestuerten Notensatz* (Mainz: Schott, 1988; ISBN 3-7957-2886-X). This publication contains both a history of metal-plate music engraving and suggestions for the implementation of traditional techniques on computer equipment. Mel Wildberger, a traditional music engraver, reviews this work in the March 1991 issue of *Notes*, pp. 805f.

Musikometrika

Musikometrika is an annual collection of articles concerned with quantitative approaches to musical information and edited by Moisei Boroda, currently a Humboldt Fellow at Bochum University. Volume 3 [ISBN 3-88339-905-1], containing articles on melody by V. K. Detlovs, M. G. Aranovskij, V. Ljublinskaja, and K. Sappok; on rhythm by Boroda; and on perception and recognition by A. Tangian, was published in the summer of 1991. Volume 4 is in preparation. Queries may be addressed to Universitäts-verlag Dr. N. Brockmeyer, Querenburger Höhe 281, W-4630 Bochum 1, Germany.

Reflections on Technology and Musicology

"Reflections on Technology and Musicology," by Eleanor Selfridge-Field, gives an overview of opportunities and needs for collaboration between technologists and musicologists. It appears in *Acta musicologica* LXII/2-3 (1990), 302ff., in conjunction with the first report of the IMS Study Group on Musical Data and Computer Applications.

Representations and Models

Computer Representations and Models in Music, edited by Alan Marsden and Anthony Pople, contains selected articles from the First International Conference on Computers in Music Research, held in Lancaster, England, in 1988. It is scheduled for publication by Academic Press, London, in 1992.

The Well-Tempered Object

The Well-Tempered Object is an anthology of articles concerning applications of object-oriented programming from the *Computer Music Journal*, 1980-89. The articles are edited by Stephen Travis Pope and published by MIT Press [ISBN 0-262-16126-5], 55 Hayward St., Cambridge, MA 02142; tel. (617) 625-8569. A number of articles describe research involving the NeXT workstation and the Macintosh personal computer; *LISP*, *Smalltalk*, and *Objective C* are among the most commonly used languages in these applications.

Bibliographical CD-ROMS

Current Contents

Current Contents on Diskette is a bibliographical database providing weekly access to the latest contents listings from leading scientific and technical journals. Associated software supports searches by title, keywords, and descriptors. Further information is available from the Institute for Scientific Information, 3501 Market St., Philadelphia, PA 19104; tel. (800) 336-4474.

The Music Index

The Music Index on CD-ROM contains approximately 200,000 bibliographical citations from *The Music Index* (1981-88), a bimonthly publication covering title and keyword information from 350 publications from 20 countries. Accompanying software permits searches by personal name, event, genre, instrument, historical period, and subject. An IBM PC compatible with MS DOS CD-ROM extensions is required. Enquiries may be addressed to Chadwyck-Healey, Inc., 1101 King St., Alexandria, VA 22314; tel. (800) 752-0515; fax (703) 683-7586.

RILM

RILM Abstracts of Music Literature, which provides 100-word summaries of articles appearing in more than 300 scholarly journals as well as books, theses, conference reports and other scholarly literature on music, is now available on a CD-ROM entitled *muse* (an acronym for MUsic SEarch). All issues from 1970 through 1984 are included, together with corrections, restoration of material lost in production, additional cross-references, and other small improvements designed to standardize the material and facilitate searching. This body of material will be captured in subsequent releases, which are to be augmented with updated material. Running on the IBM PC, *muse* is available by license on an annual subscription basis only. Enquiries should be directed to the National Information Services Corporation, Ste. 6, Wyman Towers, 3100 St. Paul Street, Baltimore, MD 21218; tel. (301) 243-0797; fax 243-0982.

CD-ROM Production Software

Several vendors offer software that enables users to edit and format ("premaster") previously stored data for storage on a CD-ROM. Search software must be provided to give users access to the reformatted data.

Knowledge Access

Knowledge Access International offers a range of electronic publishing software and services for magnetic, WORM, and CD-ROM media. Tools for the creation of CD-ROM's permit users to convert information from diverse text and graphics files and from relational database formats to a common format in which all the information is searchable and retrievable with software provided by the company. Software for the creation of desktop databases is a specialty. *KAware* authoring and indexing software for 386-PC's appears to be the least expensive product of its kind. Retrieval software to read the disk must be licensed from the company that produces the authoring software. Knowledge Access International is located at 2685 Marine Way, Ste. 1305, Mountain View, CA 94043; tel. (415) 969-0606; fax 964-2027.

Topix

Topix" for the Macintosh reads from analogue or digital audio tape, local area networks, video frames, floppy disks, WORMS, and 9-track tapes. It formats for write-once CD's, data DATS, and other media. *Topix* is a product of Optical Media International, 180 Knowles Drive, Los Gatos, CA 95030; tel. (408) 376-3511; fax 376-3519.

CD Interactive Products

Brahms's *German Requiem*

Brahms's *German Requiem* is the latest release in the *Audio Notes*" series from Warner New Media (3500 W. Olive Ave., Ste. 1050, Burbank, CA 91505; tel. (818) 955-9999; fax 955-6499). *Audio Notes* CD's are designed for use with the Macintosh II. The Brahms release features 70 minutes of digital audio, complete English and German texts, two real-time analyses of the music, a historical timeline, standard index, pronouncing index, and glossary of terms. More than 50 biographical, historical, and musical "excursions" are provided, with illustrations, as supplements. A disc of similar scope for Vivaldi's "Four Seasons" concertos is in preparation.

Consumer Tools

CD Search and Sample System

The *CD Search and Sample System* permits prospective compact disk buyers to inspect over 46,000 CD titles and to audit as many as 5000 of them by way of an in-store telephone. Searches by title, label, performer, and classification may be conducted. CDSSS is a product of Announcement Technologies, 1401 Manatee Ave. West, #3, Suite 900, Bradenton, FL 34205; tel. (813) 747-0195.

The NoteStation

The *NoteStation* is a computer-based electronic library for customized music publishing. The user may search a title list (12,000 items at last report), view the music on the screen, listen to a segment of the piece, instruct the machine to transpose it (if desired), and select parts to be printed. Selections are available in both laser-printed copies and MIDI sequences. Billing, inventory control, and royalty accounting are automatic.

Each unit contains an IBM AT-compatible PC, a CD-ROM optical storage system, and a laser printer. Pieces available are encoded and printed using Passport's *Escort* software, a sequence transcription engine for *SCORE*. The *NoteStation* is available by license through MusicWriter, Inc., 170 Knowles Dr. #203, Los Gatos, CA 95030; tel. (408) 364-2500; fax 364-2507.

Humanities Software

Oxford Text Searching System

The Oxford Text Searching System (OTSS), which is a menu-based PC interface for the mainframe version of the Oxford Concordance Program (OCP), make set texts for the study of ancient and modern literature available for online searching. Based on his use of OTSS, David Robey (Dept. of Italian, Manchester University, UK) reports on differences between Ariosto's *Orlando furioso* and Tasso's *Gerusalemme liberata* in *Literary and Linguistic Computing* 5/4 (1990), 310-3. He comments on the value of the statistics gathered in developing a broader view of "the general move from a medieval linear to a classical periodic style in Renaissance Italian literature." Enquiries about OTSS may be addressed to the Centre for Humanities Computing, 13 Banbury Road, Oxford OX2 6NN, England.

Networks

While special interest groups that meet electronically continue to multiply and thrive, a major move toward formal electronic distribution of professional news managed by learned societies and in some cases juried by editorial boards is now visible. We attempt to elucidate subtle differences of organization and purpose in the following listing.

Early Music Network

An early music network started and moderated by Gerhard Gonter early in 1991 has provided interesting reading for those with a general interest in records, books, musical events, sources, and technical matters. The subscription address is *LISTSERV@AEARN*.

BITNET. The subscription command is *SUB EARLYM-L < Your electronic address >*. The contribution address is *EARLYM-L@AEARN.BITNET.* Questions and comments may be forwarded to *GONTER@AWIWUW11.BITNET.*

EthnoForum

EthnoForum, a digest of information about work in ethnomusicology, is an online publication edited by Karl Signell at the Baltimore County campus of the University of Maryland with the help of collaborators in several other locations. *EF* is well indexed and carries discussion of a number of topics related to the integration of computers into academic life in general. In particular its considerations of a format for bibliographical citations of electronic publications, of authors' rights in dual-mode (electronic and hardcopy) publications, and of reciprocity between informal but widely distributed electronic discussion and the administration of academic societies has produced a lot of interesting reading in 1991. For details, send the message *GET WELCOME INFO* to *LISTSERV@UMDD.* Messages for inclusion may be sent to *ETHMUS-L@UMDD* with one of the following headers: *DISCUSSION, NEWS, JOBS.* Files for archiving may be sent to *SIGNELL@UMDD.*

HUMBUL

HUMBUL, the Humanities Bulletin serving British universities on *Janet*, recently was moved from Leicester University to Oxford University. The new contact address is *HUMBUL@VAX.OXFORD.AC.UK. HUMBUL* posts announcements about such subjects as symposia, grants, publications, and positions available. Stuart Lee is the editor.

IMS Network

On behalf of the International Musicological Society's Study Group on Musical Data and Computer Applications, Arvid Vollsnes is currently seeking to establish an electronic network for dissemination of information and discussion of issues confronting the field. The network would be based at the University of Oslo. Enquiries may be addressed to Prof. Vollsnes at the Dept. of Music, University of Oslo, PO Box 1017, Blindern, 0315 Oslo 3, Norway; tel. +47 245-4760; e-mail: *arvid@ifi.uio.no.*

Music Research Digest

Music Research Digest, moderated by Stephen Page, is distributed outside the United Kingdom by Peter Marvit, who has recently taken a new position. Enquiries concerning *MRD* may be sent to *music-research-request@cattell.psych.upenn.edu.* The automatic archiving system for back issues and general information has not yet been established at the new address.

Society for Music Theory Network

The Society for Music Theory began to beta-test a network for discussion of music-theoretical issues in the spring of 1991. Use of the network is intended to be available to members of the society. Enquiries may be addressed to Lee Rothfarb, Department of Music, Harvard University, Cambridge, MA 02138; e-mail: *rothfarb@husc4.harvard.edu*.

Societies

Association for Musical Art and Computer Science

An interdisciplinary association for Musical Art and Computer Science has been formed at the University of Mainz. Its members are drawn from the fields of music, musicology, computer science, mathematics, art, physics, biology, and psychology. Its objectives are to support research within this constellation of disciplines, to organize lectures on appropriate topics, and to encourage collaborative research between the university, industry, and other institutions. Organizers of the group include Prof. Dr. Christoph-Helmut Mahling (Institut für Musikwissenschaft, Johannes Gutenberg-Universität, Postfach 3980, 6500 Mainz, Germany) and Dr. Frank Wankmüller (*FRANK@UAIMZCOM.MATHEMATIK.UNI-MAINZ.DE*).

Japanese Music and Computer Society: see pp. 22-4.

Society for Music Perception and Cognition

The Society for Music Perception and Cognition was formed under the auspices of the Department of Psychology at the University of California at San Diego at the start of 1991. The objectives of the Society are "to further the scientific and scholarly understanding of music from a broad range of perspectives including [those of] music theory, psychology, psychophysics, linguistics, neurology, neurophysiology, ethology, ethnomusicology, artificial intelligence, computer technology, physics, and engineering; to facilitate cooperation among scholars and scientists who are engaged in research in this interdisciplinary field; and to advance education and public understanding of the knowledge gained." The founding board of directors, who shall initially serve for three years, consists of Edward C. Carterette, Diana Deutsch, Alain Henon, Leonard B. Meyer, John R. Pierce, Saul Sternberg, and W. Dixon Ward. Enquiries about membership and events may be addressed to Manuel Gonzales, Dept. of Psychology, University of California at San Diego, La Jolla, CA 92093; tel. (619) 534-3000.

Symposia

Computers in Music Research

The second conference on Computers in Music Research was held at Queen's University, Belfast, Northern Ireland, from April 7 through 10, 1991. Although disruptions in international travel in the preceding weeks prevented several overseas speakers from attending, a full program of talks—ranging from representation systems and data structures to analysis, cognition, instructional software, sound engineering, and ethnoacoustics—as well as an exhibit and a concert were provided. Alan Marsden organized the event. A review by Arvid Vollsnes will appear in a forthcoming issue of the *Computer Music Journal*. A handbook of abstracts is available at cost from Alan Marsden, Dept. of Music, The Queen's University, Belfast BT7 1NN, Northern Ireland, UK; tel. +44 0232-245133, X3543; fax 247895; e-mail: *A.Marsden@qub.ac.uk*.

KlangArt

A congress on the musicological dimension of music technology took place within the KlangArt Festival in Osnabrück on May 24-6, 1991. Featured speakers included Marc Leman ("The Representation of Electro-Acoustic Music"), Helmut Schaffrath ("Computer-Aided Analysis"), Christoph Lischka ("Music, Cognition, and Machines"), H. Kinzler ("The Place of Music Analysis in the World of Commercial Sequencer and Composer Software"), and Roger Dannenberg ("Computer Accompaniment and Music Understanding"). The congress was organized by Bernd Enders, who may be reached at Wilhelm-Mentrup-Weg 10, 4500 Osnabrück, Germany; tel. +49 0541-53176.

Music Perception and Cognition

The second international conference on Music Perception and Cognition will be held at the University of California, Los Angeles, from February 22 through 26, 1992. Enquiries may be addressed to Roger Kendall, Dept. of Ethnomusicology and Systematic Musicology, University of California at Los Angeles, 405 Hilgard Avenue, Los Angeles, CA 90024; tel. (213) 206-1081; fax 206-6958.

Music Printing: Past, Present, and Future

"Music Printing: Past, Present, and Future" was the title of a session held as part of the Music Library Association's annual meeting in Austin, Texas, in February 1991. Maxey Mayo discussed the past ("Letterpress Music Printing in America in the Nineteenth Century"), Cynthia Horton ("Computerized Music Engraving") and Garrett Bowles ("A Survey of PC-Based Score Programs") the present, and Mary Kay Duggan ("Paradigms for the Future").

Music Publishing and Representation

A symposium of music publishing and representation will be held at Stanford University from January 17 through 19, 1992. Featured speakers on music representation include Tom Hall, Walter B. Hewlett, Steven Newcomb, and Leland Smith. Nicholas Carter will speak on automatic acquisition of musical data.

Musical Data and Computer Applications

At its meeting in Belfast on April 11, 1991, the IMS Study Group on Musical Data and Computer Applications discussed plans to assemble a handbook of codes and languages in common use for musical applications. The handbook is now in course of preparation. The group will be formally convened at the 15th Congress of the IMS in Madrid (3-10 April, 1992) to hold a session on "New Methodologies in the Study of Melody." Participants will include Moisei Boroda, Lelio Camilleri, Helmut Schaffrath, John Stinson, Tim Crawford, and John Howard.

Theses

Several theses now in progress or recently completed are covered in detail elsewhere in this issue of *CM*.

• Larry Albright's "Computer Realization of Human Music Cognition," which was accepted for the Ph.D. at the University of North Texas in 1988, is discussed on pp. 86-9. It is available through University Microfilms International, 300 N. Zeeb Road, Ann Arbor, MI 48106; tel. (800) 521-0600 as #MCU89-00326.

• Bernard Bel defended his Ph.D. thesis, "Acquisition et représentation de connaissances en musique," in Theoretical Computer Science at Aix-Marseille III University, France in November 1990. *Cf.* pp. 78-9. Copies are available from the Group Représentation et Traitement des Connaissances (GRTC), Centre National de la Recherche Scientifique (CNRS), 31 Chemin Joseph Aiguier, 13402 Marseille Cedex 9, France.

• Uwe Seifert's *Habilitationsschrift* concerning the basis for computational musicology, "Systematische Musiktheorie und Kognitionswissenschaft: Ein Beitrag zur Fundierung der Kognitiven Musikwissenschaft," was accepted for the Ph.D. at Hamburg University in 1990; *cf.* pp. 83-5.

Japanese Music and Computer Society (JMACS) News

The Japanese Music and Computer Society (JMACS) holds several single meetings and a three-day summer symposium annually. Its main purpose is to share information about current research. A bimonthly bulletin is published in Japanese. A list of titles of talks, translated into English by Keiji Hirata, given from early in 1990 through the symposium held on August 2-4, 1991, is printed below. From these we can gain some insight into the breadth and depth of current research. The names and addresses of current officers and board members are appended.

27th Meeting   April 21, 1990
   "Case-Based Learning of Arrangement Techniques"
      T. Asaba (Recruit, Inc.)
   "From Musical Conception to Sound: Representing Music on the Computer"
      Ioannis Zannos (Research Center for Advanced Science and Technology,
      University of Tokyo)
   "Data Structure of a Sequencer and MPU-808"
      M. Yamato (Roland, Inc.)

28th Meeting   July 14, 1990
   "An Attempt at Realtime Sound-Image Control with DSP LSI"
      S. Hirano (YAMAHA, Inc.)
   "A Musical Application of SGML"
      K. Oka (Dai Nippon Printing, Inc.)
   "The Interaction between Auditory and Visual Processing when Listening to Music via Audio-Video Media"
      S. Iwamiya, K. Yamada and T. Shinbara (Kyushu Institute of Design)
   "Building a Network System for Self-Learning of Piano Performance with Automatic Pianos"
      K. Murakami and A. Hashimoto (YAMAHA, Inc.)

Summer Symposium 90   August 31 - September 2, 1990
   "Post-Representational Cognitive Models—A Case Study on Tonal Illusions"
      Y. Horii (Hitachi, Inc.)
   "A Data Structure for Automated Composition and Arrangement"
      J. Minamitaka (Casio, Inc.)
   "A Note on Computer Transcription of Sounds of Distinct Instruments"
      T. Nagatsuka, H. Katayose and S. Inokuchi (Osaka University)
   "A Computational Model of Anticipation of a Note Sequence"
      N. Saiwaki, H. Katayose and S. Inokuchi (Osaka University)
   "On the Operations of a System Supporting Cluster Technique"
      Y. Nagashima (Kawai, Inc.)

29th Meeting   October 27, 1990
  "Software Development of a Braille Score Processor"
    I. Mizutani (Osaka University of Music)

30th Meeting   December 22, 1990
  "Performer Deviation from Scores—An Examination of Ritardando and Rhythm"
    M. Yamada (Osaka University of Arts)
  "Development of a NeXT Sound Editor: O'Kinshi—A System Unifying Sound and Voice"
    N. Osaka (NTT, Inc.)

31st Meeting   February 11, 1991
  "Hyper Music Theater"
    S. Nakamura (Kyoto College of Arts)
  "Chord Description in UPIC Form"
    K. Yamanoue (Keio University)

32nd Meeting   April 27, 1991
  "Sound Design of Installation Work—Project Flash Back 1991"
    S. Hirano (YAMAHA, Inc.)

33rd Meeting   June 29, 1991
  "Demonstration and Tutorial of Macintosh Music Software: EZ Vision, Studio Vision, Sound Tools, MIDI Play, Audio Media, MAX"
    T. Tokiwano (Cameo Interactive, Inc.) and N. Takahashi (Zep, Inc.)

Summer Symposium 91   August 2 - 4, 1991
  "A System for Developing Sound Elements—O'Kinshi"
    N. Osaka (NTT, Inc.)
  "Musical Expression and the Computer"
    H. Matsumoto (Tokyo National University of Fine Arts and Music)
  "A Realtime Automated Accompanying System"
    Y. Takeuchi, N. Saiwaki and S. Inokuchi (Osaka University)
  "A Singing Computer Conducted by a Baton"
    S. Hashimoto (Waseda University)
  "The Design of Internal Data in Prolog Clausal Form for Composition and Arrangement"
    D. Nishioka (Tokyo University of Agriculture and Technology)
  "Interaction of Rhythm and Tonality on Melodic Recognition"
    S. Oomura (Hokkaido University)
  "Experiments in Piano Performance Using a MIDI Piano"
    T. Taguchi (Konan University)
  "Harmonization by Neural Networks—Implementation and Evaluation"
    N. Shibata (NEC, Inc.)

JMACS: Address List of Officers and Board Members

President:

Seiji Inokuchi
Department of Control Engineering
Osaka University
J1-1, Machikaneyama-cho, Toyonaka-shi
Osaka, 560 Japan
Phone: 81-6-844-1151 (ext. 4625)
e-mail: *inokuchi@inolab.ce.osaka-u.ac.jp*

Chief Director:

Satoshi Shimura
Osaka University of Arts
Higashi-yama, Kawanan-cho, Minami-kawachi-gun
Osaka, 585 Japan
Phone: 81-721-93-3781 (ext. 3305)
e-mail: *simura@hamamatsu-pc.ac.jp*

Board Members:

Keiji Hirata
ICOT
1-4-28, Mita-Kokusai Bldg. 21F
Mita, Minato-ku, Tokyo 108, Japan
Phone: 81-3-3456-3193
e-mail: *hirata@icot.or.jp*

Motoo Masui
Fujitsu Laboratories, IIAS
1-17-25, Shinkamata, Ota-ku
Tokyo, 144, Japan
Phone: 81-3-3730-3111
e-mail: *masui@iias.flab.fujitsu.co.jp*

Toshiaki Matsushima
IBM Research, Tokyo Research Lab.
5-19, Sanbancho, Chiyoda-ku
Tokyo 102, Japan
Phone: 81-3-3288-8477
e-mail: *matusima@trlvml.iinus1.ibm.com*

Youichi Nagashima
Kawai Gakki
200, Terashima-cho, Hamamatsu-shi
Shizuoka-ken, 430 Japan
Phone: 81-534-57-1261
e-mail: *nagasm@hamamatsu-pc.ac.jp*

Shigenobu Nakamura
Kyoto College of Arts
3-8-1, Kasugaoka, Fujiidera-shi
Osaka, 583 Japan
Phone: 81-729-55-0733

Takashi Nose
Department of Mathematical Science
Tokyo University of Agriculture and Technology
2-24-16, Nakamachi, Koganei-shi
Tokyo, 184 Japan
Phone: 81-423-81-4221 (ext. 542)
e-mail: *nose@tuat.ac.jp*

Kouichi Okumura
Ookusu High School
Kanagawa-ken, 240-01 Japan
Phone: 81-468-56-0024

Naotoshi Osaka
NTT Basic Research Laboratory
3-9-11, Midori-cho, Musashino-shi
Tokyo, 180 Japan
Phone: 81-422-59-3276
e-mail: *osaka@av-convex.ntt.jp*

Naoki Saiwaki
Department of Control Engineering, Osaka University
1-1, Machikaneyama-cho, Toyonaka-shi
Osaka, 560 Japan
Phone: 81-6-844-1191 (ext. 4627)
e-mail: *saiwaki@inolab.ce.osaka-u.ac.jp*

Takashi Suzuki
Insoft System Lab.
YAMAHA
10-1, Nakazawa-cho, Hamamatsu-shi
Shizuoka-ken, 430 Japan
Phone: 81-53-460-2485
e-mail: *suzuki@isl.yamaha.co.jp*

Kuniharu Tsuboi
Hamamatsu Polytechnic College
693, Norieda-cho, Hamamatsu-shi
Shizuoka-ken, 432 Japan
Phone: 81-534-41-4444 (key)
e-mail: *tsuboi@hamamatsu-pc.ac.jp*

Calls for Participation

• The International Musicological Society's **Study Group on Musical Data and Computer Applications** is currently assembling a handbook of musical codes to facilitate the interchange of musical data. The group would like to include, in addition to detailed descriptions of codes in extensive use for musicological applications, a series of brief descriptions of *ad hoc* codes developed for specific projects or repertories. Short commentaries citing the purpose of the code and the kinds of information represented should be sent as soon as possible to David Halperin, Dept. of Musicology, Tel Aviv University, Ramat Aviv 69 978, Tel Aviv, Israel; tel. +972 03-5450332; e-mail: *AMBROS@TAUNVM*, or Eleanor Selfridge-Field, CCARH, 525 Middlefield Road, Ste. 120, Menlo Park, CA 94025; tel. (415) 322-7050; e-mail: *XB.L36@Stanford. Bitnet*. Please include a complete address and references to any significant related literature.

• **Daniel Kastner** invites comment on his proposal that a *Music Notation Digital Interface* (*MNDI*; pron. "Mindy") standard be developed. He writes that "this standard must be in the form of a digital notation file format developed for display, printing, and MIDI implementation. With the vast array of digital storage media (CD-ROM, CD-I, CDTV, etc.) beginning to gain a market share, it is important to get a standard developed now." The standard would serve to facilitate the use of already published musical scores in these new media. It would be an open standard that would be publically documented and available to any vendor. It would make provision for uniform royalty assessment of materials made available by such digital means. Those interested in joining a consortium to develop such a standard are invited to contact Kastner at Scores International, 32 Braddock Park, Boston, MA 02116; tel. (617) 437-0222; fax 859-5943.

• **Nigel Nettheim** is conducting a survey of applications of statistics to musicology. Computer applications involving such procedures as time-series analysis, factor analysis, cluster analysis, and information theory are especially welcome. Communications may be sent to Dr. Nettheim at 204A Beecroft Road, Cheltenham, NSW 2119, Australia; e-mail: *nigel@usage.csd.unsw.oz.au*.

• **Pekka Tolonen** [*CM 1990*, p. 124] reports a new address—31 Cross Road, Wimbledon, London SW19 1PL, England; tel. and fax +44 081-543-8222; e-mail: *ptolonen@cix.compulink.co.uk*.

Byrd's Book of Notational Records: A Quiz

Developers of notational software seek examples of the most extreme cases of particular notational features in an effort to test the capabilities of their programs. While graphics software now offers means of compensating for the visual vocabulary that may be lacking in a representation system, typesetters—both traditional and contemporary—want to anticipate the complications they may encounter.

Don Byrd, a twenty-year veteran of computerized musical typography, shares with us here some items from his working list of *Extremes of Conventional Music Notation*. Readers who can improve on his working answers, which are given on pp. 122-3, are invited to submit their replies, with well documented musical proof (work names, movement names, bar numbers, and, if possible, a photocopy of the relevant passages), by July 31, 1992. The reader providing the greatest number of new records will receive a complete run of *Computing in Musicology* through 1992. Readers are also invited to submit additional questions for future issues.

Byrd notes that only published works are considered. C4 = Middle C; A0 = the lowest note of the piano; C8 = the highest note of the piano. In general, implicit notation (*e.g.*, Renaissance equivalents of complex tuplets) is excluded. Although it is notation that is mainly emphasized, some extremes of sound are also included. Suggestions for additional items and other direct queries may be sent to Donald Byrd, Advanced Music Notation Systems, PO Box 60356, Florence, MA 01060.

General

1. Longest movement (excluding dramatic works) in measures?
2. Longest movement in performance time?
3. Movement with the largest number of written notes?

Pitch

4. Most ledger lines above staff?
5. Most ledger lines below staff?
6. Highest sounding pitch?
7. Lowest sounding pitch?

Duration

8. Shortest notated duration?
9. Longest notated duration with ties?

10. Most augmentation dots?
11. Most complex tuplet?
12. Most notes/chords coupled to one beam?

Dynamics

13. Most p's?
14. Most f's?

Scoring

15. Most staves in a system?
16. Greatest number of simultaneously notated parts?
17. Most notes on a single stem?
18. Most notes in a vertical simultaneity?

Making Music

Simulated Instruments

Not so long ago electronic instrument manufacture was directed toward exploring new worlds of sound.   In recent years there has been some response to the authentic performance movement in the development of instruments designed to simulate the manual instruments of past centuries.   Correspondingly, the number of MIDI versions of traditional instruments continues to increase.   We note here examples of both kinds together with a micro-synthesizer that you can carry in your pocket or purse.

The Digital Harmonium

The *Parvus* is a single-manual MIDI keyboard instrument fashioned to look and sound like a pedal harmonium.   Its 13 stops are based on sampled sounds of organ pipes.   It is available in both portable and console versions from Gem Classical Organs U.K., 2 Brearton St., Bradford, W. Yorkshire BD1 3EA, England.

The Digital Harpsichord

The Roland C-20 and C-50 MIDI harpsichords sport settings for five historical temperaments—equal, just, meantone, Werckmeister III, and Kirnberger.   In just intonation, a tuning specific to the key of a given piece may be locally specified. Modelled on an eighteenth-century French double, the instrument provides selection of "upper" or "lower" 8-foot manuals as well as 8'/8' and 8'/4' combinations and a lute stop.   It has both fine and coarse controls for matching the tuning of live ensemble instruments.

A Kit to Digitize a Piano

For those who want to retrofit their acoustic pianos with a MIDI capability, the Solton MIDI Piano Kit offers a potential solution.   It is necessary to remove the keys in order to install the contact board.   The MIDI OUT capability enables users to connect the traditional instrument to a broad range of electronic instruments and modules.   The Solton kit is sold by Ketron S.r.l., Via G. Di Vittorio 13, 60020 Candia, Ancona, Italy; tel. +39 071-8046059.

Digital Bowed String Instruments

For those who want to generate MIDI files with a traditional violin, Zeta Music Systems will provide a VR-204 Violin RetroPak and a VC-225 MIDI violin controller (from IVL Technologies of Canada) to help do so. The RetroPak replaces the bridge and tail piece. Output from each string can be assigned to a separate electronic timbre. Zeta also provides integral MIDI violas (ZVO-204) and cellos (ZC-234) as well as MIDI guitars and guitar controllers. Zeta is located as 2230 Livingston St., Oakland, CA 94606; tel. (415) 261-1702.

A Pocket Synthesizer

The Compact Music Processor released by Yamaha as the QY10 in January 1991 combines an 8-track song sequencer, a 28-note polyphonic tone generator, a drum machine, and a keyboard pad in an 11-oz. box that measures 4" x 7⅜". Menus for 29 sampled instruments, 20 chord types (including augmented and diminished intervals and chords containing suspensions), and 76 rhythmic patterns are built in. The QY10 is intended for travelling musicians, composers, and arrangers who, once their journey is complete, can transfer files to other MIDI instruments.

Conducting Devices

Research into the development of devices that give one performer control of a synthetic orchestra has taken many routes. Although few products have so far been made commercially available, several have been demonstrated before learned societies and selected audiences. We mention here several examples.

A Baton for Electronic Conducting

An orchestral music performance system which follows the motions of a human conductor has been developed by the Ohteru Laboratory at Waseda University [this group developed WABOT, the organ-playing robot described in *CM*'s 1987 issue (pp. 84, 126) and elsewhere]. The conducting system consists of a baton-motion interpretation system (consisting of a CCD video camera and an image-point tracker), a gesture interpretation system, and MIDI instrument controllers. [The *DATAGLOVE* component is described in *IEEE Computer*, July 1991, pp. 44-53.]

Real-time performance is achieved. The system controls the tempo and expression of the musical performance, which is based on previously memorized score data, by extrapolating from baton motion and by understanding left-hand gestures (*crescendo, decrescendo, pp, vibrato*, etc.). The baton-motion and gesture-interpretation systems are able to understand some natural human gestures.

One current goal is the simulation of orchestral-performance training. This could be used by conductors as a personal rehearsal tool. The overall aim is to create not a mere "instrument" but rather a "performer" that can play with human performers in an orchestra.

The Radio Drum

Max Mathews's *Radio Drum* is a synthesizer controller which uses capacitance sensing of electromagnetic signals to continuously measure the spacial position of the drum mallets relative to a flat surface, which serves as the "drum head." Continuous tempo control of synthesized music generated from previously stored musical data may be derived from the action of beating the drum with a mallet. Other musical parameters such as timbre, volume, articulation, and vibrato may be controlled by moving a second mallet to different positions on the head. A related program supports improvisation involving the same parameters. Experiments in combining live performance with electronic conducting are currently underway. The *Radio Drum* is described is the proceedings of the *International Computer Music Conference 1989*, pp. 42-5; its origins can be traced back to 1979.

The MIDI Baton

The *MIDI Baton II*, a controller designed for synchronization, gives a human conductor control of tempo and related aspects of performances involving combined live and sequenced sources. According to its developers, it can accommodate human variance and interpretive freedom while facilitating the creation of scores "that are far broader in timbral potential and the realization of finer tolerances in pitch and rhythm control than are possible in a full symphony orchestra." Details are available from David Keane, Gino Smecca, and Kevin Wood, who are at the School of Music and the Dept. of Electrical Engineering, Queen's University, Kingston, Ontario K7L 3N6, Canada.

The *Video Harp*

The *Video Harp*" reads the shadows of a performer's fingers on a glass plate and converts the information to MIDI codes. A video harpist can perform and conduct previously stored musical information in unusual ways. According to the developers, he or she can "bow a horn or strum an organ." For further information about the *Video Harp*, which contains a Motorola 68000 microprocessor and a 3.5" disk drive, contact the Sensor Frame Corp., 4516 Henry St., Pittsburgh, PA 15213; tel. (412) 683-9500.

Musical Data

Musical data is a special interest of *Computing in Musicology* because the Center for Computer Assisted Research in the Humanities has been engaged in the development of full-score encodings of major classical repertories since 1984. There are several parallel efforts in the academic world. In the case of the CCARH, *TELETAU* (Florence Conservatory), and *ESAC* (Essen University) data bases, the information captured is a logical representation devoid of data about a specific performance but often amplified to support visual and analytical applications as well as acoustic applications that can be designed by the user.

In the past year there has been a sudden burst of commercial data sets. Generally these are MIDI transcriptions of performances, in which such things as rubatos are audible in playback. The Yamaha *Disklavier* repertory offers perhaps the best-known example of this phenomenon. The musical information has been captured from recordings, tapes, piano rolls, or newly performed sequences. In these cases it is usually possible to modify the "instrumentation" of performances or to hear only selected parts or passages, but the main emphasis is on products that are immediately usable. In essence, then, these data sets constitute new descendants of traditional recording adapted to the age of MIDI instruments.

Commercially Available Items

MIDI Hits

Bach's *Two-Part Inventions* and the first movement of Mozart's *Eine kleine Nachtmusik* are among the titles available on Passport Designs' *MIDI Hits*" sequences, which can be used with an IBM PC, Apple Macintosh, Atari ST, or Roland MC series sequencers. *MIDI Hits* are available from the Music Data division of Passport Designs, Inc., 625 Miramontes St., Half Moon Bay, CA 94019; tel. (800) 443-3210 or (415) 443-0280; fax 726-2254.

MIDI Magic

MIDI Magic" is a universal tape-to-MIDI interface that enables the user to store MIDI sequences on audio tape with an ordinary tape recorder. As a storage method, it eliminates the customary limitations of computer memory. Audio information converted to a MIDI format by *MIDI Magic* may be saved, loaded, and played again. This product is available from Micro-W Distributing, Inc., 1342B Route #23, Butler, NJ 07405; (201) 838-9027; fax 838-9090.

MIDI Song Library

The Voyetra *MIDI Song Library* is a collection of multi-track sequences that can be customized by the user. Volume 4 contains selected classical works including Chopin's "Minute Waltz," Debussy's *Clair de lune*, Beethoven's "Moonlight" Sonata, and Prokofiev's *Peter and the Wolf*. The *Library* is available in two formats—for the Sound Blaster FM Synthesizer and for the Roland MT-32/LAPC-1—and in two diskette formats, 3.5" and 5.25". Voyetra Technologies is at 333 Fifth Avenue, Pelham, NY 10803.

PianoDiscs

Fourteen disks of MIDI performances of classical piano music have been released to date in the *PianoDisc* series. One album consists entirely of performances by Horowitz and Rubinstein (of Chopin, Rachmaninoff, Brahms, Saint-Saëns, and others). Other items of note include Rachmaninoff performing Chopin (*Waltz Brillante*, Op. 34, No. 3), Schubert ("Wanderer" Fantasy), and Scarlatti (*Capriccio*); Mascagni performing Mascagni (intermezzo from *Cavalleria rusticana*); and Grainger performing Grieg (A-Minor Piano Concerto; *To Spring*, Op. 43, No. 6). Each 3.5" diskette holds one hour's worth of music. The sequence of items can be reprogrammed by the user. The diskettes work with a control box containing a menu of sampled and synthesized sounds and may be controlled remotely. *PianoDiscs* may also be used for recording and composition. Further information is available from PianoDisc, 2444 Marconi Ave., Sacramento, CA 95821; tel. (916) 973-8710.

PianoSoft Plus

PianoSoft Plus diskettes contain MIDI transcriptions of live performances suitable for simultaneous playback on the Yamaha Disklavier (simulating a piano) and the DOM-30 tone generator (simulating an orchestra). Scheduled for release in 1991 was a diskette of seventeen *Celebrated Works by J. S. Bach*. *PianoSoft Plus* diskettes are distributed by Hal Leonard Publishing Corp. of Milwaukee, WI; (714) 522-9255.

Quick Disks

The *Quick Disks* in Roland's ISM Library are intended primarily as teaching tools. In all diskettes (2.8") Track 1 is available for recording, while Track 2 contains "orchestration." Subtracks 3 and 4 contain the left- and right-hand parts of the work respectively. All tracks can be used selectively. Each *Quick Disk* is accompanied by a printed score. The diskettes work with Roland digital instruments and tone generators.

Student pianists can explore Czerny's *Progressive Studies*, Op. 139, and *Technical Studies*, Op. 849, and various Alfred Piano courses. Various works by Bach, Handel, Telemann, Scarlatti, Rameau, and Couperin are available to digital harpsichordists (see p. 25). In the Ensemble Library, which is intended for use with the MT-32 or MT-100

p. 25). In the Ensemble Library, which is intended for use with the MT-32 or MT-100 synthesizers, miscellaneous orchestral works and two piano concertos—Beethoven's Fifth (the "Emperor") and Grieg's A-Minor—are available. *Quick Disks* are available directly from the Roland Corp., 7200 Dominion Circle, Los Angeles, CA 90040 (213-685-5141) and through Micro-W Distributing, Inc., 1342B Route #23, Butler, NJ 07405; (201) 838-9027; fax 838-9090.

QRS Music Disks

QRS Music Disks for Apple, Atari, and Commodore computers include works by Satie (*Gymnopédie*), Debussy (*Arabesque*), Bizet, Bach (Prelude in C Major), Chopin (E-Minor Prelude), and other composers of recent centuries. By far the most interesting material they provide is a collection of more than 100 Gershwin songs (1916-26) performed by the composer. This material has been remastered from piano rolls to a Disklavier format using the proprietary QRS system. The disks may be used with the Yamaha MX-100. Details are available from Micro-W Distributing, Inc. [address above].

Academic Collections

The ASTRA Database

A library of pieces encoded variously in *SCORE*, *TELETAU*, and *ESAC* formats will be made available toward the end of 1991 by network using the ASTRA Database services. Remote users will be able to retrieve pieces and perform analytical tasks on the pieces provided. The service will be coordinated by the Musicological Division of CNUCE-C.N.R. at the Cherubini Conservatory in Florence. Works by Frescobaldi, Bach, Mozart, Schubert, Brahms, Joplin and many other composers have been encoded in *TELETAU* code [shown in *CM 1987*, p. 22]. *SCORE* files for such collections as Piero Gargiulo's recent edition (Florence: Olschki) of Luca Bati's Second Book of Madrigals will be made available. For information in *ESAC* files, see the next entry. Further information is available from *conserva@ifiidg*.

The Essen Databases

More than 13,000 encodings of monophonic songs have been made available to scholars by Essen University. These works, which comprise several centuries of music from German-speaking lands, are encoded in one field of an *AskSam* relational data base. They have all been encoded in *ESAC*, the Essen Associative Code. The music may be displayed, heard, searched, and analyzed using *MAPPET* and printed using *ESTAFF*, two software programs developed at the University; the text fields of the data base may also

"Der Mai tritt ein mit Freuden"

6: *REG* [Europa, Mitteleuropa, Deutschland, Niederrhein]
7: *KEY* [Z1262 08 A 3/4] ZZ [8]
8: *MEL* [-5_ 1_.231 -5_.-3 -4-5 -6_.-71-6
      -5_-4_-3_ -4_-6_-5-4 -3-51_ 3_ 321_-7_
      1__12 3_1_5_ 2_1_-7_ 1_-6_2_ -7_-5_-5_
      -6_.-71-6 -5_1_3_ 321_-7_ 1__ //]

9: *MOD* [HEPTATONIC IONIAN]
10: *ACC* [1-5_-6-5_-4-3_31_32_1-7_-6-5_31_]
11: *FOR* ['a__b__c__d__e__ev_bv_d__]
12: *FOC* ['^d_^__: a_^__^__^d_: a___]
13: *FCT* [Natur und Welt]

**ESAC code and selected input and output fields for "Der Mai tritt ein mit Freuden"
[#1262] from the Zuccalmaglio [Z] section of the Essen database of German ballads.** Field
#7 gives key and meter information. Field #8 provides the musical code. The remaining
fields are derived from Field #8 by analytical routines. Field #9 identifies the mode, Field
#10 gives a profile of pitches on the first beats of each measure, Field #11 provides a
rhythmic profile, Field #12 a structural profile, and Field #13 a description of the
associated text [which is not encoded]. [Example printed by CCARH.]

be searched. All of the material is easily disengaged from the database as ASCII text and is amenable to use with other programs. *AskSam* queries can be accessed in English, German, French, Italian, and Swedish. A brief overview of possible uses of the data is provided in Helmut Schaffrath's "Zum Einsatz von Computern in Musikwissenschaft und -pädagogik" (*Computer in der Musik*, Stuttgart, 1991), pp. 8-26. Users may also create their own files in *ESAC* code. A manual is available in German and in Peter Cooke's English translation.

The *ESAC* files and *MAPPET* software and documentation are available by license. They are free of cost to scholars. To obtain a license agreement, contact Prof. Dr. Schaffrath at the Universität Essen, FB 4 - Musik - Postfach, W-4300 Essen 1, Germany; e-mail: *JMP100@DEOHRZ1A.BITNET.*

The *Humdrum Database*

The *Humdrum Database* includes encodings of approximately 2,300 scores ranging from the twelfth-century works of the Notre Dame School to twentieth-century works no longer under copyright. More than 90 percent of the works are polyphonic. The database includes motets by Dunstable and madrigals by Morley; over one hundred works by Bach; works by Purcell, Handel, and Telemann; piano works by Beethoven, Brahms, and Satie; string quartets by Haydn, Mozart, Brahms, and Schoenberg; British folk ballads; songs by Stephen Foster; and barbershop quartets. Non-Western repertories include Balinese, Chinese, Hassidic, Japanese, Korean, Maori, Tahitian, Venda, Xhosa, and Zulu instrumental and vocal works. Further information is available from David Huron, Conrad Grebel College, University of Waterloo, Waterloo, Ontario, Canada N2L 366; tel. (519) 885-0220, fax 885-0014; e-mail: *dhuron@watservl.uwaterloo.edu.* [*Cf.* pp. 66-7.]

Program Your Own *Messiah*

CCARH cooperated with Philharmonia Baroque Orchestra and Harmonia Mundi to create a comprehensive online edition and recording of Handel's *Messiah*. Encoded material was used to produce performing scores and parts for the main work and all its variant pieces, some used in only one historical performance. These alternatives were all recorded. Users may now hear a specific version (such as the autograph version of 1741, the Dublin version of 1742, or the Foundling Hospital version of 1759) by programming the appropriate bands on the three-CD set. Lorraine Hunt, Drew Minter, Jeffrey Thomas, and the chorus of the University of California at Berkeley perform under the direction of Nicholas McGegan. The *Messiah* materials form part of the CCARH *Handel Database*.

Bibliographical and Documentary Services

L'Atelier d'Etudes de Versailles

The Atelier d'Etudes of the Centre de Musique Baroque de Versailles is currently forming five data bases intended for public access in 1992. These are designed for the use of researchers, students, and performers of early music. These data bases use the JLBDOC application program developed by the Société JLB-INFORMATIQUE. The program runs on MS DOS and UNIX machines.

The five data bases store information about works, music, names, writings, and poetry. *WORKS*, a bibliographical data base of writings after 1800 about French music and dance of the seventeenth and eighteenth centuries, currently includes more than 8000 entries. It is searchable by eight rubrics. Regine Bornefeld manages this data base and welcomes offprints and listings of information for inclusion. The *MUSIC* data base contains information about printed and manuscript sources for musical works and source concordances. It is managed by Marie Joelle Ebtinger. The *WRITINGS* data base, under the direction of Bénédict Mariolle, concerns pre-1800 documents relating to music and dance. *NAMES* is a listing of researchers, librarians, booksellers, and musicians currently involved in some way with this repertoire. *POETRY*, still under design, will serve as a tool for determining the literary sources of texts set to music.

The Atelier circulates a questionnaire to current researchers and publishes a bulletin of its activities (ISSN 0997-7872). Enquiries and bibliographical contributions may be addressed to the Centre de Musique Baroque de Versailles, 16, rue de la Paroisse, 78000 Versailles, France.

The Beethoven Bibliography Project

The Beethoven Bibliography Project maintained at the Center for Beethoven Studies at San Jose State University is identifying, describing, and indexing significant materials by and about Beethoven. The resulting database includes books, journal articles, and other published writings in and outside the field of music; first and early editions of scores; important later nineteenth-century and twentieth-century scores, and manuscripts. For rare materials, information on locations will be given. Terms used to index the materials will be maintained in a subject thesaurus, which may be browsed online or from printed copies. It is anticipated that access will be available through the SJSU Library's online public access catalogue beginning in 1992.

Patricia Elliott and William Meredith are at the Ira S. Brilliant Center for Beethoven Studies, San Jose State University, Wahlquist Library North 614, One Washington Square, San Jose, CA 95192-0171; tel. (408) 924-4590; fax 924-4365.

The EUropean Repertoire Information Service (EURIS)

The co-operation in repertoire information services, mentioned in the 1990 issue of the directory [pp. 133-7], between RIM (Repertoire Informatiecentrum Muziek, Utrecht, the Netherlands) and MusikkFunn (Sogndal, Norway) has resulted in an idea for a CD-ROM based repertoire-information system including presentation of actual score pages. It will be called EURIS (EUropean Repertoire Information System). While the present intention is to start off with a system for brass band repertoire, the idea is extendable to all kinds of repertoire.

The EURIS system will be based on the RIM model, with extensive MARC-based bibliographical cataloguing enhanced by textual comments made by musical experts on technical difficulty (including a grade between 1 and 6) and musical contents. RIM and MusikkFunn each have responsibility for collecting scores from different geographic areas. The two institutions exchange the bibliographical and textual data, thus building up two identical databases.

In addition, bit-mapped images of a selection of the score pages will be available on CD-ROM for presentation on screen. This combination of extracts of the score pages, textual comments, and a complete bibliographical description, including information on where to order scores, gives EURIS the potential of becoming a uniquely powerful tool for conductors and band leaders. Preliminary analyses indicate that the full brass band repertoire of the world, including bibliographical data, expert comments, and up to 10 scanned (and compressed) pages of each score, will fit on one CD-ROM.

In Norway, where sparse population, long distances, and, in many areas, poor transportation make it difficult for conductors to judge scores by visiting music stores or specialized music libraries, repertoire information may be more easily distributed by installing the system in public libraries. Yet by not including all pages of the score (and no single parts), illegal photocopying will be reduced. In the Norwegian model for distributing computerized band music information within the EURIS-project, the bibliographical data will be distributed to the automated catalogue at the Norwegian Music

Collection, and in this way it will be accessible for all public libraries with the necessary equipment.

As of July 1991, a prototype has been built on a Macintosh IIfx using *HyperCard*. In the prototype, all fields are searchable; any fields and any number of fields may be combined in Boolean searches, which may include numerical operators where relevant. Also, the expert comments are searchable with primitive free-text functionality. Score presentation and browsing are possible by clicking a button. In the finished system, as in the prototype, a simple user interface for the novice combined with advanced searching facilities for the professional user will be emphasized.

Dagfinn Bach (WNRC) submitted this article. Further information is available from the Repertoire Informatiecentrum Muziek, Drift 23, 3512 BR Utrecht, P.O. Box 391, NL-3500 AJ Utrecht, Netherlands; tel: +31 30-340 000; fax: 30-312 641, and from Bård Uri Jensen, Western Norway Research Centre, P.O. Box 142, N-5801 Sogndal, Norway; tel: +47-56-76 000; fax: 56-76-190.

The International Digital Electroacoustic Music Archive (IDEAMA)

The purpose of IDEAMA is to collect, preserve, and provide the broadest target collection of internationally renowned early electroacoustic music, an extremely crucial body of music composed since 1940. These works will be transferred from rapidly deteriorating analog tapes onto permanent digital storage media.

IDEAMA is a collaborative effort between two founding institutions, Stanford University's Center for Computer Research in Music and Acoustics (CCRMA), and the Center for Arts and Media Technology (ZKM), in Karlsruhe, Germany. CCRMA is an interdisciplinary facility where composers and music-technology researchers work together on a variety of projects. ZKM, founded in 1989, will house two museums for art and media technology, two institutes for art and music, archives/libraries, a videothek, and an audiothek.

To help identify, locate, and select materials appropriate for inclusion in the archive, each institution has established regional selection committees comprised of composers and other individuals who are well-versed and active in the field. Access to works from Europe, North and South America, and Asia is currently being sought. In addition to the regional selection committees, an international advisory board of individuals who have contributed significantly to the field has been formed to promote the archive's activities.

Over the next two years, approximately 500 early electroacoustic musical works will be selected for the collection based upon their historical significance and the critical deterioration of the analog tapes on which they are now stored. After this initial target collection is established, other institutions may become IDEAMA branches by housing a copy of the collection and its catalogue.

The designated works will be transferred from decaying analog recordings to permanent digital storage media, using CD standards (16-bit samples, 44,100 samples per second, two-channel stereo). In a step-by-step transferral process, the analog tape(s) on which an early work is stored will be played back on its original recording equipment. As the music is played, it will be re-recorded onto digital audio tape (DAT), where the sounds will be stored as numbers. Music now stored on the DAT copy will be "cleaned" if desired, to eliminate any unwanted clicks or pops. The digitized music will then be ready for permanent storage on compact and WORM discs. Compact discs already available will be included in the archive so that they remain available once their commercial life has expired.

Copies of music, computer-scanned scores and auxiliary materials (*e.g.,* program notes, background information) will be kept in digital form only and will be available on line. A machine-readable catalogue of the collection will be created and integrated into the RLIN and OCLC databases, as well as existing nonline catalogues at major research institutions worldwide. Once this target collection has been established, more recently composed electroacoustic music works will be added.

The technology is based on existing commercial hardware with programs designed for public access. Scholars, researchers, and electroacoustic music aficionados can browse through the searchable catalogue, which is designed to be consistent with international cataloguing standards. Semi-automatic access to archive contents will enable music selections to be heard via jukebox and/or CD players. The contents of the archive will be non-circulating. Copies will be made and distributed on DAT cassettes for scholarly purposes and in compliance with the legal rights of their owners. Since these copies will be in digital form, they will be exact replicas of the archive recordings, achieving the highest quality of sound reproduction.

Marcia Bauman, CCRMA, Department of Music, Stanford University, Stanford, CA 94305; tel. (415) 723-4971; fax: 723-8468; e-mail: bau@ccrma.stanford.edu or *Thomas Gerwin*, ZKM, Ritterstrasse 42, 7500 Karlsruhe 1 Germany; tel. +39 0721-9340-300; fax 9340-39, can provide further information.

RISM Libretto Project

Cataloguing for all librettos predating 1800 in the Albert Schatz collection of the Library of Congress, Washington, DC, has now been entered by the U.S. RISM project group at the University of Virginia and deposited in the RLIN Books file.   The nineteenth-century portion of the Schatz holdings is available on RLIN for comparison with other holdings of nineteenth-century materials. A new comprehensive guide to searching for the libretto data on RLIN is available from the project office for $2.00. The project leaders welcome comments from current users and communications from institutions or individuals with historically important collections of librettos regarding prospective participation in the project.

Marita P. McClymonds *and* ***Diane Parr Walker*** *are at the U.S. RISM Libretto Project, Music Department, Old Cabell Hall, University of Virginia, Charlottesville, CA 22903; e-mail: DPW@VIRGINIA.BITNET.*

The *Thesaurus Musicarum Latinarum (TML)*

The *Thesaurus Musicarum Latinarum (TML)*, briefly described in the 1990 edition of *Computing in Musicology* [p. 133], formally opened mainframe distribution of its database in November 1990. The database is operated by LISTSERV and a TML-FTP running on Indiana University's IBM 3090. Access to the database is free of charge.

The *TML* already includes more than half a million words of text from Latin music theory treatises written between the sixth and mid-sixteenth centuries. Currently online are over half of the Coussemaker *Scriptores*, all the Latin texts from *Greek and Latin Music Theory*, several texts from the *Corpus scriptorum de musica,* Gaffurio's *Practica musice*, texts derived from various manuscripts, and so on (published texts under copyright are used by permission of their publishers). Work is currently concentrating on the balance of the Coussemaker and Gerbert *Scriptores*, remaining volumes of the CSM, manuscript material, and earlier texts in the public domain (Boethius, Augustine, Cassiodorus, and so on). The database is intended eventually to include all published and unpublished texts.

In the *TML*, musical symbols are entered according to a table of alphanumeric codes that specify shapes, coloration, tails, ligature groups, clefs, proportions, and the like. The codes, which are largely mnemonic, are described in the TML's "Table of Codes for

Noteshapes," shown below. Complex figures, tables, and other graphic material that do not lend themselves to encoding are keyed and stored in the database as GIF-files, which can be displayed on DOS, Macintosh, and other hardware platforms. Any text contained in this material is included as part of the key; thus, intelligent searching in the *TML* will retrieve text not only from the treatises themselves but also from the accompanying graphic material. To assist searching, all text in the *TML* is very lightly normalized according to the "Principles of Orthography."

The principal TML Center at the School of Music at Indiana University has now been joined by funded centers at Princeton University, the University of Nebraska at Lincoln, the University of Colorado at Boulder, Louisiana State University, and Ohio State University. The project is directed by Thomas J. Mathiesen (Indiana University), together with a Project Committee comprised of representatives from each of the TML Centers and a ten-member Editorial Advisory Committee.

Table of Codes for Note-Shapes, Rests, Ligatures, Mensuration Signs, Clefs, and Miscellaneous Figures

Note-shape codes are placed between brackets and must appear in the order given in this table. Each group of symbols under N, P, L, or M appears together with no spaces or punctuation; each noteshape, rest, ligature, mensuration sign, clef, or miscellaneous figure is separated from the following one by a comma.

Notes		Rests	
Multiples		**P1. Multiples**	
Quadruplex	4	Quadruplex	4
Triplex	3	Triplex	3
Duplex	2	Duplex	2
Shapes		**P2. Shapes**	
Maxima	MX	Maxima	MXP
Longa	L	Longa	LP
Brevis	B	Brevis	BP
Semibrevis	S	Semibrevis	SP
Minima	M	Minima	MP
Semiminima	SMP	Semiminima	SMP
Addita	A	Addita	AP
Fusa	F	Fusa	FP

Notes, cont.

Coloration

nigra	b
vacua	v
rubea	r
semivacua	sv
semirubea	sr

Tails

cauda	c
plica	p
cauda yrundinis	cy

Direction

sursum	s
deorsum	d
dextre	dx
sinistre	sn
oblique	o

Flags

vexilla	vx
retorta	vxrt
dextre	vxdx
sinistre	vxsn

Clefs

C clef	ClefC
F clef	ClefF
G clef	ClefG

Mensuration Signs

Circle	O
Semicircle/open right	C
Semicircle/open left	CL
Semicircle/open top	CT
Semicircle/open bottom	CB
Rectangle	R
Triangle	TR

Proportions

A line of *diminutio* is indicated by "dim" following mensuration symbols. Fractional proportions are indicated numerically (*e.g.*, 3/2).

Ligatures

Ligatures are indicated by "Lig" followed by a series of symbols for the number of notes, the coloration, the side on which the tail appears, and the intervals included (with "a" for ascending and "d" for descending).

A descriptive brochure about the TML may be obtained from **Tom Mathiesen**, *TML Project Director, Department of Musicology, School of Music, Indiana University, Bloomington, IN 47405; email: MATHIESE@IUBACS.BITNET or MATHIESE@UCS.INDIANA.EDU).*

The *Dance Figures Index*

American Country Dances (1730-1810), the first publication in the series *Dance Figures Index*, employs a coding system to facilitate systematic analysis and computer-assisted statistical study. Robert Keller is the author. The basic figures of each dance are listed by title and gesture (*e.g.* "hands across") as well as entered in code. They are listed sequentially by page from the source. In all, 2,738 dances and 83 sources are presented.

Previously offered by The Hendrickson Group, the *Dance Figures Index* is now distributed by Pendragon Press, RR1, Box 159, Stuyvesant, NY 12173. *American Country Dances* is available both in paperback [ISBN 1-877984-04-3] and on disk as a *Dbase* file.

Music Theory Index

The *Music Theory Index*, a bibliographical work to be published by Pendragon Press, covers writings, especially in harmonic theory, from the late Renaissance to about 1935. It will contain a comprehensive listing of the published books and articles in English that pertain to the field of music theory. Fifteen thousand entries are anticipated.

The database that provides the foundation for this project is being constructed using *FoxBASE+/Mac*™ on a Macintosh SE. The data entry system requires physical examination of each item included. The software is compatible with versions of the same program running on the IBM PC and compatibles, and with other relational database software, such as *dBase IV*. The possibilities of offering online access to the *Music Theory Index* and/or a CD-ROM edition are under consideration. Completion of the project is planned for 1994.

Chronological codes allow for access to theoretical information referring to particular style periods in music history. Composer and work lists facilitate Boolean searches (*e.g.*, Schenkerian analysis [subject heading] of works by Chopin [composer list]). Key word requests, from a current listing of 1250 theoretical terms, plus other general musical terms, will enable the location of very specific technical data.

Norman L. Wick *is Assistant Professor of Music Theory at the School of Music, Southern Methodist University, Dallas, TX 75275; tel. (214) 692-3632.*

Applications in Historical Musicology

The Melodic Grammar of Aquitanian Tropes

Determining the extent to which the melodic style of the Aquitanian repertory is stable and unified is a major goal of the present study. Other goals are (1) to analyze the melodic style of tropes, in comparison with their companions, the introits; (2) to explore whether this melodic style is shared by at least one other Aquitanian chant repertory or is limited by geographic, temporal, and genre-related boundaries; (3) to hypothesize the content of a working (albeit elementary) grammar for this repertory; and (4) to use statistics established by this study to attempt to reconstruct an introit trope from the neume shapes alone, without regard to heighting, and so to understand more about the music and the method.

The introit trope melodies (with their texts) found in the Paris manuscript Latin 1119 were entered into a computer database. The method of encoding was designed to provide both a final printed copy of the tropes in modern chant notation (using *SCORE*), and a set of data for statistical analyses. Each neume shape was assigned a letter of the alphabet, or a combination of letters, and was treated as an integral unit. In the two settings of the same chant text shown below, neumes 7, 12-14, and 16 diverge:

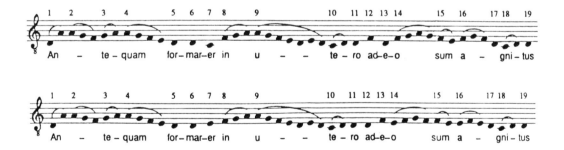

Computer programs in *Turbo Pascal* analyze the data and provide statistical summaries. Additional programs sort the neumes by type and pitch and provide a summary of the initial pitches for the individual neumes. The local intervallic relationships between neighboring neumes are categorized by the computer. A word dictionary, containing an alphabetical list of the words in the tropes with their associated neumes and pitch assignments, provides the foundation for reconstructing melodies. Other programs analyze the relationship of the structural notes to the accents in the text, and also consider punctuation in order to correlate the grammatical structure of the text with the melodic cadences.

The two statistical tools used to explore the question of a consistent, integral, and stable melodic style were chi-squared analysis [to compute the numerical significance of the results] and discriminant analysis [to minimize the chance of misclassification]. Both tests are computed with a standard commercial computer program, *SAS (Statistical Analysis System)*.

A systematic method to reconstruct neumes from the neume types and text alone was developed. Probability matrices for each neume type and each relationship between two neumes were made. The probability matrices can be modified further to reflect text accents, text-painting, and syntax. There is a matrix for each neume and the connection between any two successive neumes. These matrices can be multiplied together by the computer, and the computer determines the most probable melody. This program is also written in *Turbo Pascal*.

REFERENCES

Binford-Walsh, Hilde M. "The Ordering of Melody in Aquitanian Chant: A Study of Mode One Introit Types," *Cantus Planus, Budapest, 1990* (IMS Study Group on Chant), pp. 327-39.

Hilde M. Binford-Walsh is completing a doctorate in music at Stanford University. She would be happy to provide additional information or software source code as an aid to others engaged in similar research. She can be reached at 89F Escondido Village, Stanford, CA 94305; tel. (415) 497-5299.

Texts for the Propers of Time of Cambrai Cathedral

A current project to reconstruct the texts to the Propers of Time of Cambrai Cathedral, 1250-1550, as they are found in surviving antiphoners and breviaries of the church, uses the database developed in Hungary for use in the project *Corpus Antiphonalium Officii Ecclesiarum Centralis Europae (CAO-ECE)*. It is particularly suitable for comparative work.[1] Dufay was one of the most eminent composers who worked in Cambrai. The recent discovery of new material by Dufay gave impetus to the the idea of trying to identify chants newly composed for Cambrai and to examine attribution possibilities for anonymous chants.

With the *CAO-ECE* database, it is possible to type the contents of each source into a file and compare the sources, thereby reconstructing the Cathedral's liturgy and isolating any changes that occurred. Together with separate study of the music and of pertinent archival documents, this project will facilitate the documentation of a history of liturgical change and of chant composition (or compilation) at the Cathedral. The database will not be available for on-line consultation, but the files will be published in hard-copy along with a short introduction to the Cathedral liturgy and the contents of the database on diskette, perhaps in 1992.

---

[1] A similar database, *CANTUS*, developed by Ruth Steiner at the Catholic University of America, provides detailed indices of antiphoners but is less suitable for comparisons of sources. *CAO-ECE* and *CANTUS* both use *dBase*.

REFERENCES

Dobszay, L. "The Program *CAO-ECE*," *Studia Musicologica Academiae Scientiarum Hungaricae*, 30 (1988), pp. 355-360.

Dobszay, L. and G. Proszeky. *Corpus Antiphonalium Officii-Ecclesiae Centralis Europae: A Preliminary Report* (Budapest, 1988).

Barbara H. Haggh *is in the Department of Music, University of Maryland Baltimore County, 5401 Wilkens Ave., Catonsville, MD 21238; tel. (301) 465-5250; e-mail: HAGGH@UMBC.BITNET. She can provide assistance in obtaining the CAO-ECE materials cited.*

Byrd's Manuscript Motets: A New Perspective

The English composer William Byrd (d. 1623) was the most prolific composer of his generation, exploiting virtually every genre favored by Elizabethan and Jacobean musicians. His legacy includes a large corpus of liturgical music, covering both the Latin and Anglican rites. Virtually all of Byrd's Latin church music was published during his lifetime in editions of unimpeachable authority. However, several additional Latin motets have survived with attributions to Byrd.

The recently completed project comprised a computer-assisted analysis of nine motets which survive only in manuscript and which are of doubtful authorship (although all have at some time been attributed to Byrd). The project involved an exhaustive computer-assisted stylistic comparison of the *bassus* parts of the nine pieces with the *bassus* parts of all Byrd's Latin sacred music published between the *Cantiones Sacrae* (1575) and the Mass for Five Voices (*c.* 1595). Over eleven thousand tests were carried out on each piece, covering such features as melodic contour, durations, text setting, phrase structure, and rest patterns. As a result, conclusions are drawn as to the likelihood of each of the nine pieces having been composed by Byrd. The findings will be published in November 1991 in celebration of the 450th anniversary of Byrd's birth.

REFERENCES

Morehen, John. "Byrd's Manuscript Motets: A New Perspective" in *Byrd Studies*, ed. Alan Brown and Richard Turbut (Cambridge: Cambridge University Press, 1991), pp. 51-62.

Morehen, John. "Computer-Assisted Musical Analysis: A Question of Validity," *Proceedings of the International Computer Music Conference 1986* (San Francisco: Computer Music Association, 1986), pp. 337-40.

John Morehen is in the Department of Music, University Park, Nottingham, NG7 2RD, England; tel. +44 0602-484848, X.2052; fax 420825; e-mail: John_Morehen@vme.nottingham.ac.uk or AMZJM@VAX.CCC.NOTTINGHAM.AC.UK.

International Inventory of Villancico Texts

From the sixteenth through the nineteenth centuries, villancicos were performed in matins of Christmas, Epiphany, and on other feasts in religious institutions throughout the Hispanic world. Text booklets, or *pliegos sueltos*, containing as many as ten separate villancicos, frequently were printed for these services. More than three thousand examples of these sources survive in libraries and archives in European countries, and in the Americas. In addition, thousands of villancicos remain in manuscript in Hispanic archives. In the *International Inventory of Villancico Texts* these sources are being organized in three files: (1) bibliographic information on *pliegos sueltos* (including library and call number, institution, feast, year, composer, printer); (2) incipits from each section of villancicos in the *pliegos sueltos*; (3) textual incipits from each section of manuscript villancicos. The files share a unique code for each *pliegos suelto*. As of July 1991, there were over 5000 incipits combined in the first two files. A presentation on the database was made at the Annual Meeting of the American Musicological Society in Oakland, California, in November 1990, and the first fruits of research on the database will be unveiled in presentations at the International Musicological Society in Madrid, Spain in April, 1992.

The database is currently being used to identify textual concordances (for which a fourth file has been started) and the pairing of texts with music manuscripts, although other applications are possible. Scholars studying Hispanic music will find the database valuable in placing individual villancicos, or bodies of works, into an historical context. The project is being done through VMS on the VAX cluster at the University of Denver Computer Center. The machine in use is a VAX 8350 and the data-processing program is *SAS*.

David Martinez lives in Lima, Ohio, and **Paul Laird** is from the University of Denver. Access to the database may be gained by contacting Paul R. Laird, Lamont School of Music, University of Denver, 7111 Montview Blvd., Denver, CO 80220; tel. (303) 871-6400; e-mail: PLAIRD @DUCAIR.BITNET or PLAIRD@ATHENA.CAIR.DU.EDU.

The Music of Domenico Zipoli

Domenico Zipoli (1688-1726) was an Italian-Argentine composer whose music is being reevaluated in light of bibliographical discoveries made in Latin America since 1950. Although the composer, who is noted in histories and anthologies for his keyboard music, worked as a missionary among native populations in South America, his continued career there as a composer of Baroque music is largely unnoticed.

A recently completed research paper for a Master's degree in library science includes a biographical essay, a bibliographical essay on modern writings in Spanish about the composer, and a citation analysis based on these secondary sources. To promote both access and use as a reference tool, the translations of the Spanish materials are included in an appendix and are available from the author in machine-readable form. Two hypertext engines, *Guide* and *Hytext*, have been explored as possible engines for presentation of the material collected.

Mark A. Crook, who is willing to provide ASCII files for inclusion in personal databases, is at OCLC, Inc., 6565 Frantz Road, Mailcode 232, Dublin, OH 43017-0702; tel. (800) 848-5878.

A Database of Sources for Italian Monody

A full-text database of all manuscript sources of Italian monody to c.1630, with melodic incipits, is currently under development at the University of Illinois. The database also includes texts from certain groups of monody prints, libretti of stage works, and literary sources, *e.g.*, Guarini's *Il pastor fido*. Its purpose is to locate concordances and to identify text sources. *Savvy PC* is used for the study of text paraphrase.

John Walter Hill can be reached at 2136 Music Building, University of Illinois, 1114 W. Nevada, Urbana, IL 61801; tel. (217) 333-0371; e-mail: HILL@UIUCVMD.BITNET. Savvy PC is a discontinued product of Excalibur Technologies, 122 Tulane St., Albuquerque, NM 87106; tel. (505) 265-1273.

A Database of Vivaldi Arias

A full-text database of all arias included in all productions of all operas with which Antonio Vivaldi is known to have been associated is in formation at the University of Illinois. Beside full poetic text, each record includes opera title, city, year, season, theater, composer, poet, singer, personage, act, scene, number, musical sources, and melodic (pitch) incipit. Associated programming, using *Savvy PC*, locates likely instances of text paraphrase. The purpose is to find clues to reused arias in the absence of surviving scores. This, in turn, will serve to assess Vivaldi's conception of the relationships between aria, text, music, and libretto in a broader study of Vivaldi's operas. The database is also useful for identifying the contents of aria miscellanies.

REFERENCES

Hill, John Walter. "Vivaldi's *Griselda*," *Journal of the American Musicological Society,* 31 (1978), 53-82 [reprinted in the *Garland Library of the History of Western Music*].

Hill, John Walter. "Vivaldi's *Orlando furioso:* Sources and Contributing Factors" in *Opera and Vivaldi*, ed. Michael Collins and Elise K. Kirk (Austin: University of Texas Press, 1984), pp. 327-46.

Hill, John Walter. "A Computer-Based Analytical Concordance of Vivaldi's Aria Texts: First Findings and Puzzling New Questions about Self-Borrowing" in *Nuovi studi vivaldiani: Atti del Convegno Vivaldi 1987* (Florence: Olschki, 1988), pp. 511-534.

Hill, John Walter and Tom Ward. "Two Relational Databases for Finding Text Paraphrases in Musicological Research," *Computers and the Humanities*, 23/4 (1989), 105-111.

John Walter Hill is at 2136 Music Building, University of Illinois, 1114 W. Nevada, Urbana, IL 61801; tel. (217) 333-0371; e-mail: HILL@UIUCVMD.BITNET.

Handel's Keyboard Music:
A Computer Analysis of Style and Taxonomy of Characteristic Figures

The aim of this study is to develop a database comprising the entire corpus of Handel's music for solo keyboard, with full critical apparatus, in machine-readable form so that (1) the style can be thoroughly analyzed by comparing or relating any combination of musical variables (including contextual data); (2) the composer's vocabulary of figures and their combinations can be studied in terms of their basic "chemistry," characteristic formations, associations, etc.; (3) the music can be systematically compared, at various analytic levels, with that of other composers who might have influenced or imitated Handel; and (4) the resulting database, research methods, and technology will provide a positive contribution to the advancement of Handel studies and computational musicology.

The advent of the computer has raised hopes that our remarkable ability to distinguish one composer or composition from another would finally be explicated and mechanically simulated. Based upon an established record of successful analysis, both manual and computational, of Handel's music, this project would be significant, first, as an attempt at a systematic and exhaustive analysis of an entire musical genre of a major composer; secondly, as pioneering research in the methods and techniques of computational musicology; and, thirdly, as a major step towards the realization of a dream that was science fiction only twenty years ago: the creation of a machine that can store, analyze, document, display, classify, compare, retrieve, reorganize, print, perform, and perhaps finally imitate the work of any composer.

Graham Pont *is at the University of New South Wales, PO Box 1, Kensington, New South Wales 2033, Australia.* ***Nigel Nettheim*** *is at 204A Beecroft Road, Cheltenham, New South Wales 2119, Australia; nigel@usage.csd.unsw.oz.au.*

The Music of Michel Richard de Lalande

The music of Michel Richard de Lalande (1657-1726) is the basis of three computer initiatives of several years' standing. First, scores of previously unedited works are being prepared with *Professional Composer* and *Finale* on a Macintosh SE. Several such works were performed during the *Journées Lalande* at Versailles in September 1990. Second, a series of analytical and statistical studies has been undertaken using *Filemaker Pro*. Third, a thematic catalogue, prepared in cooperation with the Centre de Musique Baroque de Versailles [*cf.* p. 33], is nearing completion. *Finale* and *Quark XPress* have been used in its creation.

Lionel Sawkins can be reached at 6 Aldersmead Road, Beckenham, Kent BR3 1NA, England; tel. +44 081-778-2877; fax 071-733-8779. He would be interested to hear from others engaged in similar projects using the same or alternative software.

Register of Musical Data in London Newspapers

The team effort to produce a *Register of Musical Data in London Newspapers (1660-1800)*, reported in previous issues of *CM* [*e.g., 1990*, p. 136], has continued vigorously over the past year. As information is collected, its strengths and weaknesses come into clear perspective, providing a basis for determining how best to proceed. A decision was made this year to extract all references from the papers included but to restrict the collection of data to the main newspapers of the time. While it has been determined that the data cannot be relied upon as a calendar, its availability in large quantities in machine-readable form will help to eliminate the present duplication of effort and to prevent errors and omissions resulting from lack of access to a broad, comprehensive range of information. It is hoped that an index for the period 1660-1720 will be available early in 1992.

Rosamund McGuinness is in the Music Department, Royal Holloway and Bedford New College (University of London), Egham Hill, Egham, Surrey TW20 0EX, England; tel. +44 0784-443532, fax 437520; e-mail: UHWM001@VAX.RHBNC.AC.UK.

Simulation of Historical Repertories

Gregorian Chant and Medieval Monody

The generation of pieces in the style of Gregorian chant has been accomplished using a feature-extraction technique called *finitely inductive sequence (FIS) processing*. The repertory, which was selected to represent a "natural sequence of acts already written in symbolic notation," was first processed to produce an "experience base." The rule-base, aimed at determining what the next note in any specified musical context is likely to be, was created by factoring ten examples in parallel. Many of the "patterns" derived from the [numerically encoded] pitches correspond to neumes. For example, the derived rule that the fourth note in a series beginning with two ascending major seconds followed by a descending major second is likely to be followed by a descending major second corresponds to the neume *podatus bisubpunctis*.

In a second phase of the work, the system was offered the opportunity to compare monophonic songs by Machaut with the chant material and was successful in recognizing the second repertory as being different from the first, particularly in its greater use of chromaticism and its cadential formulae.

The generation of new pieces was accomplished in a third phase, by concatenating short phrases. An example follows:

REFERENCES

Fisher, Paul. "Finitely Inductive Sequence Processing," *Bulletin of Mathematical Biology*, 46 (1984).

Novaes, Marcos, Paul Fisher, and George Mobus. "Pattern Recognition and Generation in Music," *Abstracts of the ECAI Workshop on Artificial Intelligence and Music, Stockholm, August 7, 1990* (coll. Antonio Camurri).

Marcos Novaes, Paul Fisher, and *George Mobus* carried out this research in the College of Arts and Sciences, Dept. of Computer Science, University of North Texas, Denton, TX 76203; tel. (817) 565-2767; e-mail: novaes@dept.csci.unt.edu.

A Tool for Research on Improvised Counterpoint

The common view holds that improvisation cannot be studied systematically for lack of a written record and that there could not be a method for improvisation apart from primitive or rigid formulas. The goal of the present research is to re-interpret the original counterpoint treatises in the hope of uncovering some methods by which fabled improvisors of the past might have created music of legendary artistry. A rigorous method with reproducible results was sought to extend my experience in training students and professional musicians. Computer simulation has become a tool for validating these research conclusions.

A simulator of Renaissance instructions on modal counterpoint as they might have been applied extemporaneously in practice is currently being developed in the programming language *C*. It allows the user to vary the rules, the order in which rules are acquired and applied by the performers, and the precedence to observe when conflicting rules apply. The simulator allows the user to reconstruct a sequence of steps in learning counterpoint analogous to an actual apprenticeship and to compare the musical results of changing any aspect of the method. The repertory for the project is the polyphonic art music composed around 1500.

The simulator knows the procedures, the structural melodies upon which the counterpoints are improvised, the vocabulary of florid contrapuntal patterns, and the relation-

	Gama ♮ quadrati	Gama nature	Gama ♭ mollis
Γ	8 10 12 13 / ut mi sol la	12 13 15 / re mi sol	15 17 19 / re fa la
A	8 10 12 / re fa la	10 12 13 15 / ut mi fa la	13 15 17 / ut mi sol
B	6 8 10 / ut mi sol	10 12 13 / re fa sol	12 13 15 17 / ut re fa la
C	5 6 8 10 / ut re fa la	8 10 12 13 / ut mi sol la	12 13 15 / re mi sol
D	5 6 8 / re mi sol	8 10 12 / re fa la	10 12 13 15 / ut mi fa la
E	3 5 6 8 / ut mi fa la	6 8 10 / ut mi sol	10 12 13 / re fa sol
F	3 5 6 / re fa sol	5 6 8 10 / ut re fa la	8 10 12 13 / ut mi sol la
G	1 3 5 6 / ut mi sol la	5 6 8 / re mi sol	8 10 12 / re fa la
a	1 3 5 / re fa la	3 5 6 8 / ut mi fa la	6 8 10 / ut mi sol
b	-3 1 3 / ut mi sol	3 5 6 / re fa sol	5 6 8 10 / ut re fa la
c	-3 1 3 / re fa la	1 3 5 6 / ut mi sol la	5 6 8 / re mi sol
d	-5 -3 1 / ut mi sol	1 3 5 / re fa la	3 5 6 8 / ut mi fa la
e	-6 -5 -3 1 / ut re fa la	-3 1 3 / ut mi sol	3 5 6 / re fa sol
f	-6 -5 -3 / re mi sol	-3 1 3 / re fa la	1 3 5 6 / ut mi sol la
g	-8 -6 -5 -3 / ut mi fa la	-5 -3 1 / ut mi sol	1 3 5 / re fa la
aa	-8 -6 -5 / re fa sol	-6 -5 -3 1 / ut re fa la	-3 1 3 / ut mi sol
bb	-10 -8 -6 -5 / ut mi sol la	-6 -5 -3 / re mi sol	-3 1 3 / re fa la
cc	-10 -8 -6 / re fa la	-8 -6 -5 -3 / ut mi fa la	-5 -3 1 / ut mi sol
dd	-12 -10 -8 / ut mi sol	-8 -6 -5 / re fa sol	-6 -5 -3 1 / ut re fa la
ee	-13 -12 -10 -8 / ut re fa la	-10 -8 -6 -5 / ut mi sol la	-6 -5 -3 / re mi sol

The Contrapuntist's Hand as charted by Guillaume Guerson in *Utilissime musicales regule....* , 3rd edn. (Paris, 1518), Book II, Part One, f. B.v.ᵛ. This table shows both the solmisation of contrapuntal patterns, or *palmae*, within each hexachord and the size of the interval formed with the tenor note shown to the left.

ships contained within *The Contrapuntist's Hand* [see illustration on p. 52]. Each of these elements is a parameter which may be independently varied prior to a simulated improvisation of a two-voiced counterpoint so that the outputs of successive simulations may be readily compared.

The musicological goal of the computer simulation is to demonstrate that early manuals on counterpoint contain a method for training musicians to improvise advanced florid counterpoint using the elements of hexachordal solmisation, the forerunner of modern *solfegge*. The study aims to show that modal counterpoint can be successfully modelled and simulated to advance our understanding of contrapuntal techniques and learning methods. The proof lies in the artful and reproducible musical results from running the simulator.

In addition there is a need to create a test bed for comparing differing interpretations of contrapuntal rules and procedures by allowing multiple trials of each interpretation. This approach helps to establish what rules are essential and in what order they must be applied in order both to optimize mastery of the material and to create satisfying musical results.

The benefit of this research to other scholars lies in showing how discrete event simulation can be applied to studies of musical processes. When completed, the software system could be made available as program listings or as ASCII text files on diskettes or other magnetic media. Output files from the simulator could be printed as "improvised" counterpoints with an accompanying explanation.

This work is the only one of its kind and this project differs from much computer-based research in that the computer is the learning subject, rather than the master, as found in most CAI programs. To reflect the dynamic processes of counterpoint as musicians actually created it, the simulation environment is based on a discrete event simulation of dynamic systems, rather than a rule-based expert system.

Timothy C. Aarset is at the Massachusetts Institute of Technology, Lincoln Laboratory, 244 Wood Street, Lexington MA 02173; tel. (617) 981-0499.

Simulating Melodies in the Style of Bach

CONCERT is a recurrent network architecture used to generate new melodies in the style of melodies presented in a training set. It is trained using a variation of what is called the back-propagation algorithm; this facilitates next-note prediction based on probabilities derived from the events in the training set. In the composition phase, each note generated by use of a transition table is tested against the probability table. Certain notes can be predicted on the basis of local structure, while others require a global knowledge of the context. The upper voice of ten short keyboard pieces by J. S. Bach was used for a training set. The aims of future research include more precise representation of pitch, introduction of rhythmic data, and exploration of the concept of hierarchical context units.

REFERENCES

Ellman, J. L. "Finding Structure in Time," *Cognitive Science*, 14 (1990), 179-212.

Kohonen, T. "A Self-Learning Musical Grammar, or 'Associative Memory of the Second Kind'," *Proceedings of the 1989 International Joint Conference on Neural Networks*, 1 (1989), 1-5.

Krumhansl, Carol L. *Cognitive Foundations of Musical Pitch*. New York: Oxford University Press, 1990.

Mozer, M. C. "A Focused Back-Propagation Algorithm for Temporal Pattern Recognition," *Complex Systems*, 3 (1989), 349-81.

Mozer, M. C. "RAMBOT: A Connectionist Expert System that Learns by Example" in *Proceedings of the IEEE First Annual International Conference on Neural Networks*, ed. M. Caudill and C. Butler. San Diego: IEEE Publishing Services, 1987.

Shepard, R. N. "Geometrical Approximations to the Structure of Musical Pitch," *Psychological Review*, 89 (1982), 305-33.

Michael C. Mozer *is in the Department of Computer Science and the Institute of Cognitive Science, University of Colorado, Boulder, CO 80309-0430; e-mail: mozer@boulder.colorado.edu.*

Reviving *Don Giovanni* with *EMI*

The Subjects of Dr. Lustgall may be the first opera in which the principal character is a musicologist. In the libretto by Claudia Stevens, Dr. Lustgall seeks to lure Mozart's Don Giovanni back from the nether world and into the present. The music to which the work will be set is being composed by David Cope's *EMI* [*Experiments in Musical Intelligence*] *SoundsLike* program. The opera will be performed at the University of Richmond, Virginia, in the spring of 1992.

SoundsLike, which is written in *Lisp* and runs on Macintosh computers, creates its own rules of composition from music it has analyzed. Small elements of musical passages ["signatures"] from a score are assembled in a dictionary of sorts. Then items from it are selected and recombined, using an augmented transition network, to create a new work. The process has been termed "recombinant" in some recent publications. Although *SoundsLike* can create a new work on the basis of only two stored and analyzed pieces in the desired style, the results are more convincing when the number of stored works and available signatures is larger.

The accumulating contents of the lexicons being created for the recomposition of *Don Giovanni* for *Dr. Lustgall* and other works by Mozart suggest that many signatures are unique to particular periods of the composer's activity. It is hoped that Mozart scholars will pursue these clues to Mozart's idiomatic development. To whom (or what) historians will credit the music for *Dr. Lustgall* remains to be seen.

While we cannot provide a preview of the new work, we can offer, as a supplement to last year's coverage of *EMI*, a few bars from a Scott Joplin piano rag composed by the *SoundsLike* process. *EMI* [discussed in *CM 1990*, pp. 122-3] has also been used to simulate Palestrina masses, Bach inventions, Chopin mazurkas, and Scriabin preludes.

REFERENCES

Cope, David. "Recombinant Music: Using the Computer to Explore Musical Style," *IEEE Computer*, 24/7 (July 1991), 22-8.

David Cope *is at Porter College, #88, University of California, Santa Cruz, CA 95062; tel. (408) 423-2418; e-mail: howell@ucscd.uscs.edu. He has recently completed the composition of **The Well-Tempered Disklavier**, a cycle of 48 preludes and fugues for soloist and/or interactive human/electronic use, and the writing of **Computers and Musical Style** [cf. p. 9].*

Conclusion of a piano rag in the style of Scott Joplin
as composed by David Cope's *EMI SoundsLike* program.

Applications involving Tablatures

TabCode for Lute Repertories

A project to facilitate the cataloguing of music written for the lute and related instruments whose form of notation was tablature is currently underway at King's College, University of London. An important aspect of the work is to decide on an ASCII-based encoding format for lute tablatures, so that data can conveniently be exchanged and transferred to the data-structure used by the software that is in development. The same coding system could also be used for printing or as a means of integrating lute tablature into musical or text documents (for instance, for thematic catalogues). The system under development is called *TabCode*.

Tablatures of various types for lutes and many other instruments have existed almost as long as notated music, but the focus of this research is on the European lute, whose written repertory roughly spans the 16th-18th centuries. Even this requires the accommodation of a dozen or so different varieties of instruments, and a more-or-less indefinite range of tuning possibilities, although a few favorite tunings can be regarded as defaults. Tablature notation itself existed in various forms for different instruments, at different times, and, above all, in different countries. But the basic principle remained the same, and it is regarded as axiomatic for the present research that the various styles of lute tablature can all be reduced to a single universal code which can conveniently be represented in machine-readable form.

Unlike conventional musical notation, tablature does not aim to notate the pitch and duration of notes in the music, but rather to indicate to the player the left-hand fingerboard positions and the sequence and timing of the right-hand strokes which produce the notes. In this sense, since there is basically nothing "abstract" about the notation, it is well suited to computer treatment, although there are complicating factors, such as a vast array of idiosyncratic and usually context-dependent ornament symbols which may or may not affect the "basic musical content" of the material.[1]

For the purposes of bibliographic cataloguing, any coding system has to be capable of representing a diplomatic facsimile of the source; for less exacting types of research, a more modest degree of faithfulness to the original may suffice. Thus a full encoding

---

[1]For example, while a sign indicating vibrato does not affect the "basic musical content" but simply the manner of performance, one indicating an appoggiatura might do so. In fact, it is common for sources to differ in this latter respect, one using a sign where another uses an extra note; the implications for the algorithmic recognition of concordances are obvious and non-trivial.

(in *Full TabCode*) will need to contain details (specifying exact positioning, which may be relevant in any context-sensitive case) of any text or symbol attached to any part of the tablature page (including titles, marginal comments, underlaid lyrics, etc.), all ornament and technical signs (including lines, slurs and non-standard signs), fingering numbers and symbols, ink colors (red tablature symbols sometimes had special significance) and more besides. Much of this may be nonessential detail for other types of data-processing, such as transposition, melodic pattern-matching or full-scale concordance-recognition or analytical work. For these purposes an encoding of the essential data (in *Minimum TabCode*), giving the notes, rhythm-signs, barlines, time-signatures, etc., will suffice. In the present state of development, *Full TabCode* comprises *Minimum TabCode* plus the detailed level of information enclosed (at the relevant point) within parentheses.

It is intended that it will not be necessary for the user/cataloguer to learn the encoding system, since a simple graphical user-interface will provide the means to record lute tablature to a sufficient level of complexity. It is desirable, however, that the encoding system retain a close relation to the original notation, so that it can easily be edited manually, should the need arise. Like any encoding system it should be unambiguous and precise, flexible and comprehensive, yet sufficiently economical that large amounts of music, or large numbers of musical incipits, can be stored and/or processed without incurring severe overheads.

Although the development work is being carried out on Macintosh computers, whose graphical user interface (GUI) is especially well suited to this sort of application, the coding system will be machine-independent, using the limited character-set of standard ASCII, without Macintosh (or IBM) extensions. As well as causing fewer problems of confusion arising from "special" characters, this will mean that data can be exchanged using standard file transfer techniques or normal electronic mail without difficulty.

Example of *Tabcode* representations of early 17th-century French tablature are shown below.

Nicolas Vallet, *Secretum Musarum* II (1616), No. 1, p.1, "Ballet A.9."

Full TabCode representation (755 chars):

> T(RX3: 41 39 36) MC | Q.a1b2d3a5 Ed2. Qb2:, a2,d6 | d3(C1:-45) b6
> Ea6 a7 Hc3(C-1:4)c4a6 | Ed3a5 a2. Qb2: Ed2d6 a1.-6(C2:5) b1:
> d1-2.-3(C-2:5) | Ha1b2b3d5 Xa1 | Ea1a5 d3. a1: d2. b2: d3. a2: b3. |
> d4(C3:67) d3. a2: d3.-4(C-3:7) c3c4(C4:67) d3. a2: c3.-4 (C-4:67) |
> d3d4-5(C5:5) a2. b2:(C6:-25) c4(C-5:4) d2(C-6:4)a4 a1. Qb1a2 |
> Ha1b2b3d5 QXa1(C7:32) Ea1:-3(C-7:7) c1. | Qd1a2 E-1 (C8:-20)c4 a3
> Q-2(C-8:2)b3 Ed2:-3(C9:36) a1.-2(C-9:7) | Qb1d2d3. E-1(C10:-20)a4 c4
> Q-1(C-10:0)d4 Eb2:-4(C11:26) d2.-3(C-11:8) | Qa1d5 Ed2a4 b2. a2c4 d3.
> Qa2c3a6 | Hd3c4a5 QXa2 Ec4:a3. | Qb3: E-3(C12:-40)a6 c6
> Q-3(C-12:0)d6(C13:48) Ea4: c4-6(C-13:5) | Qd4: E-4(C14:-35)a7 a6
> Q-4(C-14:4)b6 Ed5:-6(C15:37) a4(C-15:7) | c4: Xa1 d3(C16:35) a7
> c3(C-16:4)a6 d3. Qa2: | Hd3c4a5 Xa2 |(34)

Minimum TabCode (408 chars):

> MC | Q.a1b2d3a5 Ed2 Qb2 a2d6 | d3b6 Ea6 a7 Hc3c4a6 | Ed3a5 a2
> Qb2 Ed2d6 a1 b1 d1 | Ha1b2b3d5 Xa1 | Ea1a5 d3 a1 d2 b2 d3 a2 b3 |
> d4 d3 a2 d3 c3c4 d3 a2 c3 | d3d4 a2 b2 c4 d2a4 a1 Qb1a2 | Ha1b2b3d5
> QXa1 Ea1 c1 | Qd1a2 Ec4 a3 Qb3 Ed2 a1 | Qb1d2d3 Ea4 c4 Qd4 Eb2 d2
> | Qa1d5 Ed2a4 b2 a2c4 d3 Qa2c3a6 | Hd3c4a5 QXa2 Ec4a3 | Qb3 Ea6 c6
> Qd6 Ea4 c4 | Qd4 Ea7 a6 Qb6 Ed5 a4 | c4 Xa1 d3 a7 c3a6 d3 Qa2 |
> Hd3c4a5 Xa2 |

Encodings of Vallet's "Ballet."

This piece takes up two lines; Vallet's book has a total of 287 lines of music in its 50 pages. So a complete encoding of the book would require approximately 105.8 kilobytes (108342.5 bytes) for *Full TabCode* or 57.2 kilobytes (58548 bytes) for *Minimum TabCode* (*i.e.*, *c.* 2 Kbytes per piece).

The design of *TabCode* is by no means frozen, and suggestions, criticisms, and improvements will be welcomed. A draft description of *TabCode* (with examples) is available by post or e-mail.

Timothy Crawford *is at the Department of Music, King's College, University of London, Strand, London WC24 2LS, England; tel. +44 071-836-5454; e-mail: t.crawford@oak.cc.kcl.ac.uk.*

ERATTO Software for German Lute Tablatures

The capabilities of ERATTO software for the automatic transcription and analysis of German lute tablatures, which was originally developed from 1968 to 1980 in collaboration with Henri Ducasse, have been extended since 1986 with the help of Bernard Stepien, an information specialist in artificial intelligence and a researcher at the University of Ottawa. Work with French guitar tablatures, reported in the following article, was initiated in collaboration with ERATTO.

A new concept of software related to the process of musicological analysis enables us today to obtain far more satisfying results on musical structure and/or framework than were previously possible. We are finally able to go from obtaining a simple "translation" of characters, as in the 1970's, to an automatic structured transcription which displays the polyphonic organization of musical text.

The current status of work as of the beginning of 1991 can be demonstrated with three instructive pieces taken from the collected works of Hans Newsidler, *Der ander Theil des Lautenbuchs*:

> 1. "Ein seer guter Organistischer Preambel," f° Aiij v° [shown with the original source in *CM 1988*, p. 99].
> 2. "Disant adiu madame," f° Biij [shown in *CM 1990*, p. 147].
> 3. "Ein gut trium mit schönen fugen," f° Diij v° [shown on the following page].

These works demonstrate a sampling of the problems involved in resolving this type of transcription: in the first, in representing simple counterpoint; in the second, in studying the copying of short cells; and in the third, of long imitations and frequent overlapping. The correct detection of themes and imitations and their differentiations in fortuitous series of similar notes is the most difficult of the undertakings. At the start, all similarities are detected and listed. The musicologist must select the meaningful ones. Application to the appropriate voice (upper, middle, or bass) is then automatic. The process is explained in the accompanying illustration. Transcriptions of the works are soon to be published.

Eighty percent of the work done today is completed automatically. We hope in the near future to be able to achieve a more complete automatic transcription process. Nevertheless, we expect that about 10% of the work will be left to musicologists to interpret, since the precise nature of the informational science does not allow for interpretation, in a reasonable time, of those harmonies, unisons, and rests that do not relate to a specific program but rather reflect the intentions of the composer.

10. EIN GUT TRIUM. MIT SCHONEN FUGEN

```
============================================================
IMITATION DETECTEE ! transposée a l'unisson.
a la mesure: 36 vert. :1 vs  mesure: 36 vert. :2
      fa2   fa2   sol2 la2   sib2 fa2   sol2 la2   do3  do3  sib2
ref: 202   204   205  206   207  208   209  210   212  213  214
      fa2   fa2   sol2 la2   sib2 fa2   sol2 la2   do3  do3  sib2
imit:203   206   207  208   209  210   211  212   215  217  218
essaie assigner # 8
theme # 8 nombre total d'imitations = 2
inspection affectation imitation manquante # 1
1 manquante a trouvé une solution a la voix N° 2
inspection affectation imitation manquante # 2
2 manquante a trouvé une solution a la voix N° 2
toutes les imitations ont été inspectées
============================================================
```

ERATTO software for the detection of points of imitation.

In the above example, each rhythmic event has a number. In Bar 36 the event numbers are 202-4, in Bar 37 they are 205-8, in Bar 38 they are 209-212, and in Bar 39 they are 213-219. In the analysis at the top of the page the pitches of the bass voice are above the row of event numbers marked "ref:" and the pitches of the middle voice are above the event numbers marked "imit:". While rests and ties are ignored here in seeking matches, pitch repetitions are observed. The difficulty of the exercise is in locating fuzzy matches. In this example the "match" [*la do*] between the bass events 210-(211)-212 [circled] and the middle voice events 212/215 [circled] is a non-literal match involving consecutive quarter notes on adjacent pitches vs. tied quarter notes (on the same pitch).

To set up this software, we have specially chosen a general microcomputer easily accessible to the musicologist who is a non-specialist: we use an IBM PC XT or compatible, 640K memory, with a Hercules graphics card, a graphics terminal, and a graphics laser printer. The musicologist can thus achieve at home an environment which will allow him to test his hypotheses and see the results of his work. Certain more complex aspects of these problems will nevertheless require the use of more sophisticated materials and systems such as Sun or NeXT workstations, which at present are only available in highly specialized laboratories.

This version of the software is available for Macintosh computers with Michel Wallet's software *Euterpe* with additions by musicologists for unisons and rests.

Hélène Charnassé is based at ERATTO, C. N. R. S., 27 rue Paul Bert, 94200 Ivry-sur-Seine, France; tel. +33 49-60-40-45; fax 49-60-40-80. Bernard Stepien is at 183 Crestview Road., Ottawa, Ont. K1H 5G1, Canada; e-mail bernard@uotcsi2.bitnet.

French Sixteenth-Century Guitar Tablatures:
Transcriptions and Analysis

A frame-based and rule-based expert system for automatic transcription of French sixteenth-century guitar tablatures into standard notation has been developed at the Ecole Nationale Supérieure de Télécommunication de Bretagne, in Brest, France.

The task of transcribing tablature, like that of translating Chinese poetry into English, may appear unnecessary as it involves a considerable amount of interpretation and therefore some loss of information. However, just as everyone does not read Chinese with ease, so the number of those who can read and play directly from old tablatures is rather small. In addition, Renaissance four-course guitars are rare nowadays. Furthermore, tablature is not a musical notation and therefore it does not provide an adequate representation to study or analyze musical structures and rules of composition of this period.

Rules implemented in the expert system for dance transcription were defined by Madame Charnassé, a musicologist at the ERATTO research group at the Centre National de Recherche Scientifique in Paris. Using these rules, inferences are made by the computer to:

- transcribe the notes, given the tuning of the guitar
- detect enharmonic notes and suit them to the musical context
- determine the best tuning (of three) for the work
- choose whether one plays both strings of the course together or the upper octave string alone
- search for the upper melodic line and the bass line
- determine the rhythmic value of each note in this voice

Finally, the result is represented in a two-stave format. Notes that do not belong to the upper voice are shown as white notes without stems.

Guitar tablature (a) and two-stave transcription (b) differentiating principal melody [in black] from remaining tones [in white] from a dance by Adrian le Roy (1551).

An output format will soon be available for Michel Wallet's *Euterpe* software for music printing (*cf. CM 1990*, p. 65).

The *Y3* frame-based system was chosen to design this dynamic knowledge base for tablatures and scores. *YAFOOL*, the kernel of *Y3*, is implemented on the *Le-Lisp* system. This hybrid system also contains the *PRYSM* inference engine based on production rules, the *FYLTRE* pattern-matching tools and the *YAFEN* graphical user interface. This interface allows the visualization of application behavioral evaluation and therefore makes prototyping easier. Development of this software takes place under *UNIX* on a Sun4/Sparc workstation.

Input is in the form of an ASCII file describing the tablature's physical structure. A related part of the project concerns the automatic acquisition of printed tablature from scanned materials in the *Cinq livres de guitarre, 1551-1555* of Adrian le Roy and R. Ballard (Monaco: Edition Chanterelle, 1979).

Denise Derrien-Peden, Ioannis Kanellos, *and* **Jean-François Maheas** *can be reached at the Ecole Nationale Supérieure de Télécommunication de Bretagne, Groups Intelligence Artificielle et Systèmes Cognitifs, BP 832, 29285 Brest Cedex, France; tel. +33 98-00-14-54; fax 98-00-12-82; derrien@ensth-bretagne.fr.*

Representation and Analysis Software

Programs for musical analysis, as well as those for composition and pedagogy, involve the manipulation of musical data. Although the end results may be quite different, the means by which the data is represented or reorganized may be conceptually similar. Integrated systems to support these and other diverse functions, such as music printing and sound synthesis, abound. The more facets a system has, the more difficult it is to report, because multiple representations or interpretations of musical data may be used to support these diverse ends.

Recognition of the importance of music representation grows in proportion to the number of application programs available for use. Since the representation of music is substantially more complex than the representation of text, task-oriented programs are usually machine-specific. Portability across platforms remains more a goal for the future. *CM* has provided substantial coverage of methods of music representation (*1987*, pp. 1-22) and of efforts to devise standards for the interchange of musical information across hardware platforms (*1989*, pp. 26-8, and *1990*, pp. 51-8). Subsequent coverage of these topics is supplementary to earlier articles.

The intellectual models pursued in analysis continue to increase in number. Our age seems to be an experimental one, in which the possible value in music applications of countless numbers of concepts and procedures drawn from mathematics, statistics, computer science, artificial intelligence, and neurobiology is considered. Communication between practitioners of these diverse disciplines and of musicology remains difficult, not only because what is considered elementary in one may be quite foreign in another but also because what is valued in one may be paid slight regard in another. To avoid the inherent risks of distortion and disciplinary chauvinism, we have refrained from translating the terminology of one field into that of another. We have, however, taken the liberty in the following sections of abridging discussion that presupposes knowledge that may not be general to most of our readers. In this section contributions are ordered roughly by platform, beginning with UNIX (including NeXT) workstations, then moving on to applications for Macintosh, MS DOS, and Atari microcomputers.

Humdrum: Music Tools for UNIX Systems

Humdrum is a system by which music-related data can be represented and coordinated. For the most part, it is oriented toward common musical notation. However, *Humdrum* provides representation and analysis tools that permit users to represent a variety of notations including lute tablatures, ethnomusicological symbols, electroacoustic note lists, conducting gestures, and dance notations. [A substantial quantity of material has been encoded; this is reported on p. 32.]

The musical elements represented include enharmonically distinguished absolute pitch, duration (including N-tuplets), phrasing, slurs, ties, tempi, most ornamentation and articulation, barlines, meters, tempi, keys, key signatures, stem direction, beaming, dynamic markings, and text underlay/overlay (by extension). Encoding methods include facilities for encoding non-Western systems of tuning, performance mannerisms, tablatures, etc., as well as analytic representations such as functional harmony and psycho-physical representations such as critical bands.

The *Humdrum* system provides an unlimited context through which unorthodox or unusual classes of objects can be represented in a lucid and inter-compatible form. Represented objects might include manuscript watermarks, handwriting characteristics, stochastic meta-scores, sound synthesis patches, performance bio-mechanics, seating arrangements, etc. Apart from the representation system itself, the *Humdrum* software tools reflect analytic emphasis on perceptually related music research. Other investigators have used *Humdrum* to pursue set-theoretic work, studies in functional harmony, rhythm, and studies in conflicting attributions.

The *Humdrum Toolkit* is a set of some 50 interrelated software tools intended to assist in the representation and analysis of musical notation. All software tools are written in *awk* and/or *C* and are designed to work in conjunction with standard UNIX software tools. With these tools it is possible to produce tabular synopses of such phenomena as voice crossings, contrapuntal motion, parallel motion, intervallic proximities within or between voices, and melodic motion by direction or interval. Queries of arbitrary complexity can be constructed.

The generality of the tools may be illustrated through the *Humdrum* pattern command. The *pattern* command supports full UNIX regular-expression syntax. Pattern searches can involve pitch, diatonic/chromatic interval, duration, meter, metrical placement, rhythmic feet, articulation, sonorities/chords, dynamic markings, lyrics, or any combination of the preceding as well as other user-defined symbols. Moreover, patterns may be horizontal, vertical, or diagonal (*i.e.*, threaded across voices).

Two encodings of Bar 52 of the Andante moderato from Brahms's String Quartet No. 2, shown on the next page, illustrate (a) the basic input code and (b) a metrically padded representation:

a:

```
    !! Rehearsal marking 'E'
    =52      =52      =52      =52
    4CC#     8F#      4c#      4G#
    .        8D#      .        .
    8r       8E#}     4r       4r
    {32C#    {32c#    .        .
    32BB     32B      .        .
    32AA     32A      .        .
    32GG#}   32G#}    .        .
    4FF#     8F#      8r       8.r
    .        {32a     {32cc#   .
    .        32g#     32b      .
    .        32f#     32a      16cc#
    .        32e#}    32g#}    .
    8.r      8f#_     8a_      4ff#
    .        32f#     32a      .
    .        32en     32g#     .
    16FF#    32dn     32f#     .
    .        32c#     32e      .
    =53      =53      =53      =53
```

b:

```
    !! Rehearsal marking 'E'
    =52      =52      =52      =52
    4CC#     8F#      4c#      4G#
    .        .        .        .
    .        .        .        .
    .        8D#      .        .
    .        .        .        .
    .        .        .        .
    8r       8E#}     4r       4r
    .        .        .        .
    {32C#    {32c#    .        .
    32BB     32B      .        .
    32AA     32A      .        .
    32GG#}   32G#}    .        .
    4FF#     8F#      8r       8.r
    .        .        .        .
    .        .        .        .
    .        {32a     {32cc#   .
    .        32g#     32b      .
    .        32f#     32a      16cc#
    .        32e#}    32g#}    .
    8.r      8f#_     8a_      4ff#
    .        .        .        .
    .        .        .        .
    .        32f#     32a      .
    .        32en     32g#     .
    16FF#    32dn     32f#     .
    .        32c#     32e      .
    =53      =53      =53      =53
```

Humdrum is written in *awk* [a *C* prototype] and *C*. Since *awk* may be cross-compiled to *C* using a UNIX utility [*awkcc*], *Humdrum* may be ported to any machine that supports a *C* compiler. At the University of Waterloo, *Humdrum* is used on Sun SPARC servers running UNIX and PC's running DOS.

*scor [pron. "star-score"] is a *Humdrum* representation of visually rendered notation suitable for printing works in common musical notation.

David Huron *is at Conrad Grebel College, University of Waterloo, Waterloo, Ontario, Canada N2L 366; tel. (519) 885-0220, fax 885-0014; e-mail: dhuron@watserv1.uwaterloo.edu.*

Keynote: A Language for Algorithmic Applications

Keynote is an *awk*-like programming language and graphical editor for MIDI data, with both algorithmic and realtime applications. Version 4 is now available in the AT&T System Toolchest. The graphical interface is based on only a few built-in functions. The entire user interface of a complete music editor (piano-roll style with pop-up menus) is written in *Keynote* itself and is hence completely customizable and extensible by the user. Although it works best on UNIX systems with X Windows, *Keynote* is portable and runs on the Macintosh and Amiga. An archive-server has been set up to allow for sharing of documentation and music. A manual, a quarterly newsletter, and source code are all available to users.

Tim Thompson can be reached at AT&T Bell Labs, Room 3C-231, Crawford's Corner Road, Holmdel, NJ 07733; tel. (908) 949-4339; e-mail: tjt@twitch.att.com.

LabanWriter 2.2 for Choreographic Notation

A new release [Version 2.2] of *LabanWriter*, a program to facilitate the creation of choreography, will be released this autumn by the Department of Dance at Ohio State University. Differences between this edition and version 2.1 [shown in *CM 1990*, pp. 110-1] include the addition of buttons in the main palette and of text on the page. Version 2.1 improved on Version 2.0 in supporting the resizing of symbols on the page, the automatic numbering of measures, and the ability to drag staves in page layout.

LabanWriter software is free of cost. It does require a Macintosh Plus or higher model, and a hard disk is strongly recommended. The developers require that the program be distributed only with its complete manual. For those who wish to receive upgrades as soon as they are ready, an annual subscription ($30/year) is available.

To obtain the most recent version of *LabanWriter*, send a blank, double-sided 3.5" disk to the address given below. Subscribers should make checks payable to Ohio State University, Department of Dance.

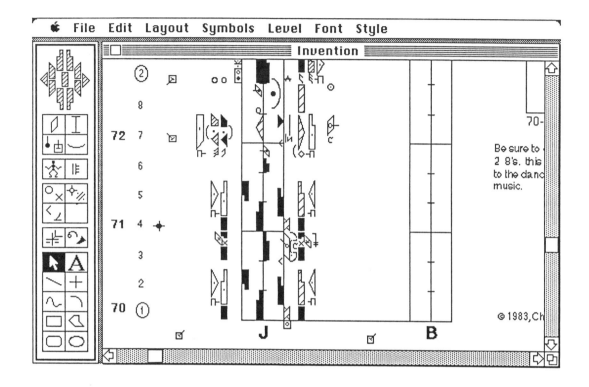

Used by permission.

LabanWriter: An excerpt of Doris Humphrey's "Invention" (1949); notation by Terri Richards (1983).

Scott Sutherland, *a developer of LabanWriter, may be reached at Ohio State University, Department of Dance, 120 Sullivant Hall, 1813 N. High Street, Columbus, OH 43210; tel. (614) 292-7977; e-mail: scott@dance.ohio-state.edu. Technical support is also available from* **Lucy Venable**, *whose article on the project will appear in* **Dance Research**, *IX/2 (1991), at the same address; e-mail: lucy@dance.ohio-state.edu.* A copy of **LabanWriter** can be obtained via anonymous file transfer protocol from ftp@dance.ohio-state.edu.

Nutation: An Object-Oriented Notational System for the NeXT

Nutation is a music notation system under development at Stanford University's Center for Computer Research in Music and Acoustics (CCRMA). In *Nutation*, the images and conventions of particular notational styles take the form of data encapsulated as object specifications in an object-oriented, visual programming language. Objects in the system display a specifiable graphics image. They are characterized as much by this image as they are by their state and behavior.

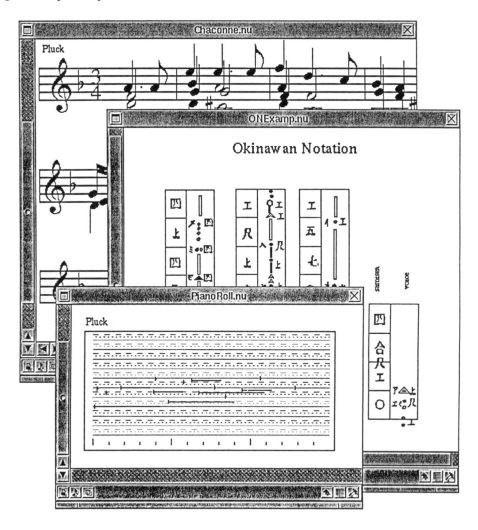

Samples of three kinds of notation—conventional Western, Okinawan, and piano roll—created with *Nutation* are shown in overlapping windows on a NeXT computer.

The system uses a consistent visual metaphor in which two-dimensional musical scores are seen as three-dimensional constructs made of piles of objects. Equivalent to tree structures, these piles specify hierarchical relationships defining temporal ordering among their component objects. Manipulation of these piles is equivalent to manipulation of their temporal ordering.

Nutation is being developed on the NeXT computer, and is capable of high-quality, real-time audio playback of its scores using the machine's on-board digital signal processing hardware. Its main aim is to facilitate composition.

REFERENCES

Diener, Glendon R. "Conceptual Integrity in a Music Notation Program," *Proceedings of the International Computer Music Conference, Glascow, 1990* (San Francisco: CMA Publications, 1990), pp. 348-50.

Diener, Glendon R. "Modeling Music Notation: A Three-Dimensional Approach." Ph.D. Thesis, Stanford University, 1991.

Glendon Diener, CCRMA, Dept. of Music, Stanford University, Stanford, CA 94305-8180; tel. (415) 723-5203; grd@ccrma.stanford.edu.

Threader: A Tool for Encoding and Analysis Using *Prolog*

A program to support flexible graphic-oriented input and editing of musical scores, particularly those of the twentieth century, is under development in a Macintosh II microcomputer running the Advanced AI System *Prolog* interpreter. This project has three purposes: (1) to develop a universal list-based data structure that can be used with languages such as *Lisp* and *Prolog*;[1] (2) to develop a knowledge-based program shell to aid in facilitating high-level AI-based analytical inquiry; and (3) to develop a graphic-oriented input device to facilitate quick and flexible input of a musical score or excerpt.

---

[1] Although this data structure is similar to that of Alexander Brinkman (*Journal of Music Theory*, 1986), his requires all scores to be input in the *DARMS* encoding language and to work in a *Pascal* environment. The declarative-based knowledge models of such AI languages as *Lisp* and *Prolog* provide new opportunities for the implementation of analytical routines.

The input device uses a chromatic grid system for placement of events within a time-space grid. Clicking the mouse at a starting location prompts the user with information about duration. A second click on the same event elicits a pop-up menu of choices enabling the modification of that event. Information that can be entered in DARMS code can be appended to the event. Once a score is entered, events may be selected and "threaded" together to form user-defined analytical objects. These objects can then be manipulated in any manner programmed in the *Prolog* inference engine.

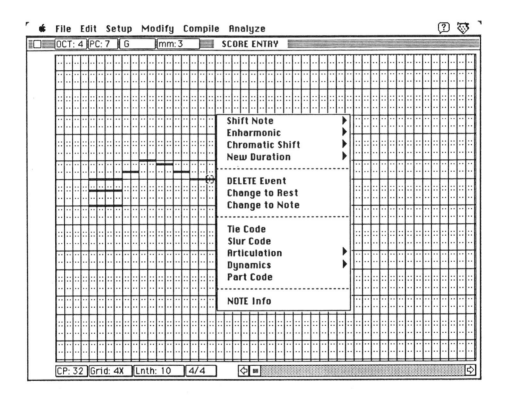

Threader: Sample input screen.

John William Schaffer, *who edits the annual* Computers in Music Research, *is at the School of Music, University of Wisconsin-Madison, 455 North Park Street, Madison, WI 53706; tel. (608) 263-1900; e-mail: jwsaesss@wiscmacc or jwsaesss@vms.macc.wisc.edu.*

Contemporary Music Analysis Package (CMAP)
for the Macintosh

The *Contemporary Music Analysis Package* (*CMAP*) is an extensive collection of tools to aid in set-theoretic analysis of atonal and serial music. *CMAP* provides functions to analyze and manipulate pitch-class sets and pitch-class rows, to analyze K/Kh relations, and to calculate invariance relations among collections of pitch classes.

The original version of *CMAP* was developed by Craig Harris and Alexander Brinkman to run on the UNIX operating system. Many characteristics of the *CMAP* package—such as implementation of the functions as a package of small, separate programs, and dependence upon the piping of filter programs to provide a flexible set of analysis tools—reflect this heritage.

One of the primary concerns during the design stage of the *CMAP*'s adaptation to the Macintosh was to incorporate the functions provided by the original tool set in a unified Macintosh-like user interface. Most functions of *CMAP* on the Macintosh are available through an Analysis Scratchpad. This is a window in which pitch-class combinations can be entered, analyzed, and transformed. Set information is displayed in "analysis lines," which show the set-class name, prime form, interval vector, and other related information for the pitch classes entered. Commands are provided to generate sets; to test set classes for properties of invariance and interval content; and to perform transformations such as transposition, complement and union.

Two methods have been found for dealing with functions such as those involving row matrices, set complex tables, subset relations, and pitch class mapping, which provide information which does not fit into the Analysis Scratchpad. First, certain commands simply attach a comment on to an analysis line. For instance, "Count Pitch Classes" appends a table of the frequency with which each pitch class appears in a tone row. As an extension of this idea, the user is also able to append comments to lines in the Scratchpad. This can be an aid in referencing sets to a musical work being analyzed.

Certain commands provide more information than that which can be conveniently displayed as a comment to an analysis line. For these commands additional windows were designed. These include a "row matrix" window, in which pitch class and pitch-order matrices can be generated. The user can also search for the occurrence of specific sets contained in the matrix. Other windows have been designed to generate tables of K/Kh relations ("set complex window"); to show operations under which a set maps into itself or into an arbitrary superset ("set mapping window"); and to analyze vertical structures created by segmenting and overlapping rows ("rotational array window").

The UNIX version of *CMAP* requires the user to enter pitch-class data using hexadecimal notation. Although this is an extremely efficient way of entering data, many users prefer to view musical data in other formats. The Macintosh version of *CMAP*

Set complex window for calculating K/Kh relations.

		4-8	4-9	8-15 4-15	5-6
	4-8				Kh
	4-9				K
8-15	4-15				Kh
	5-6	Kh	K	Kh	
7-7	5-7	Kh	Kh	K	
	5-19	K	Kh	Kh	
6-38	6-6	Kh	Kh	K	K
	6-13		K*	K*	
	8-28				

supports duodecimal notation, decimal integers, and pitch-class names; MIDI keyboards are also supported for data entry. The notation used during data entry may be converted to another format if the user so wishes.

All versions of *CMAP* are conceived as tools for interactive analysis. In order to provide a fast and efficient implementation of the various software tools, a database of set-class information is stored in an extremely compact form which remains resident in memory. Sets are stored as bit vectors. This keeps memory usage to a minimum and allows for the implementation of particularly efficient algorithms for all operations. The Macintosh version of *CMAP* provides a comprehensive set of tools for set-theoretic analysis, unifying a collection of thirty separate programs into one unified application. Priority has been given to implementing fast algorithms using compact data representations.

REFERENCES

Castine, Peter. "The Development of Computer-Based Set-Theoretic Music Analysis Tools," *Computers in Music Research Conference Handbook* (Belfast: The Queen's University, 1991), pp. 25-7.

Castine, Peter, Alexander R. Brinkman, and Craig R. Harris. "Contemporary Music Analysis Package (CMAP) for Macintosh" in *Proceedings of the 1990 International Computer Music Conference, Glascow, 1990* (San Francisco: CMA Publications, 1990), pp. 150-152.

Harris, Craig R., and Alexander R. Brinkman. "An Integrated Software System for Set-Theoretic and Serial Analysis of Contemporary Music," *Journal of Computer-Based Instruction*, 16/2 (Spring 1989).

Harris, Craig R., and Alexander R. Brinkman. "A Unified Set of Software Tools for Computer-Assisted Set-Theoretic and Serial Analysis of Contemporary Music" in *Proceedings of the 1986 International Computer Music Conference*, San Francisco: Computer Music Association, 1986.

Peter Castine is at the Technische Universität, Sekretariat H51, Straße des 17 Juni 135, Berlin, Germany; e-mail: pcastine@mvax.kgw.tu-berlin.de. All versions of CMAP are available from Alexander Brinkman, Eastman School of Music, 16 Gibbs Street, Rochester, NY 14604.

MacGAMUT Software for Melodic Dictation

The newly released *Melodic Dictation* module of *MacGAMUT*, a MIDI-compatible aural-training program for the Macintosh, contains over 1,000 melodies organized into 18 levels of difficulty. Each student exercise is randomly organized from the melodies in a given level and is presented in a key and clef randomly selected from the choices set by the instructor. The instructor may change, delete, or add to the given melodies, and may re-order the given levels or add new levels. The student may enter the melody on a MIDI keyboard; pitches, durations, and rests will be displayed on the screen. The music may also be entered and edited using a mouse. Answers may be compared both aurally and visually. *Melodic Dictation* is programmed in *THINK Pascal*, using the *MacGAMUT* Music Courseware Development System developed by Ann K. Blombach and a pitch representation system based on work by Walter B. Hewlett.

REFERENCES

Blombach, Ann K. "Tools for Macintosh Music Courseware Development: Hewlett's Representation System and Structured Programming," *Journal of Computer-Based Instruction*, 16/1 (Winter, 1989).

Hewlett, Walter B. "A Base-40 Number-Line Representation of Musical Pitch Notation," forthcoming in *Musikometrika*, 4 (1991).

Ann K. Blombach *is at the School of Music, Ohio State University, 1858 Neil Avenue, Columbus, OH 43210; tel. (614) 292-1026; e-mail TS0183@OHSTMUSA.* **MacGAMUT: Melodic Dictation** is available from Mayfield Publishing Company, 1240 Villa Street, Mountain View, CA 94041; tel. (800) 433-1279.

MacMusicLogo

MacMusicLogo is a computer environment and a collection of open-ended projects for developing musical thinking, hearing, and appreciation. With full access to the procedural power of *Logo*, students can design higher level musical structures and immediately hear them performed by the four to eight separately programmable "voices" and a selection of "instruments" chosen from either the internal synthesizer of the Macintosh, which has been enriched, or a MIDI-compatible external synthesizer.

A variety of graphic representations of musical procedures is also available. Each highlights a different aspect of the same musical configuration. Comparative examination of procedural description, graphic representations, and music apprehended often reveals surprising similarities and differences. For example, the structural trees shown below

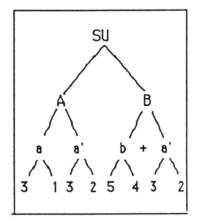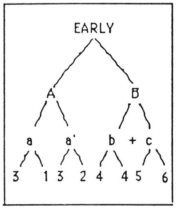

facilitate comparison of the procedural similarities and differences between Stephen Foster's "Oh, Susanna" [SU] and the English folk song "Early One Morning" [EARLY].

Conversely, using a series of melodic phrases, students may experiment with sequence and repetition to determine what combinations produce music that seems to be "finished."

Moving between media and between description and perception, students are encouraged to develop the capacity to represent musical phenomena in multiple ways. The process of discovering that multiple representations and multiple hearings of the same work are possible and that one may selectively choose among them becomes a primary source for learning, for designing, and for reflection on the artistry of musical invention.

Jeanne Bamberger, who was on leave in 1991 at the Institute for Research on Learning (2550 Hanover St., Palo Alto, CA 94304), is in the Department of Music, Massachusetts Institute of Technology, Cambridge, MA 02139.

COMES: An Integrated *Smalltalk* System

COMES, a Computer-Supported Workstation for Musicians, is a music software system under development at the Institute for Musicology in the University of Mainz, Germany. The intention is to link application components (for example, for score editing, analysis, and pedagogy) with a core component to facilitate various routine tasks performed by musicians. A single data structure will be used for these diverse applications.

The emphasis during the current phase of the research is to develop a method of music representation that is flexible enough to store a wide range of different information about musical pieces. A basic syntax has been completed. In the next phase this syntax will be implemented, using *Smalltalk 80*, and application modules will be developed.

Frank Wankmüller is at the Institut für Musikwissenschaft, Johannes Gutenberg-Universität, Postfach 3980, W-6500 Mainz, Germany; tel. +49 6131-392259; e-mail: Frank@UAIMZCOM. MATHEMATIK.UNI-MAINZ.DE. *Cristel Mittelbach* is at Projekt COMES, FB 17, Universität Mainz, Postfach 3980, W-6500 Mainz, Germany; e-mail: CHRISTEL@UAIMZCOM. MATEMATIK.UNI-MAINZ.DE.

Polymetric Processing with BP2

The *Bol Processor*, Version 2 (*BP2*), deals with polyphonic structures of sound-objects represented with arbitrary symbols. It is an extension of software developed by Bernard Bel and Jim Kippen in the early mid-1980's to examine improvisatory methods used by North Indian tabla drummers (Marsden and Pople, 1991).

The polymetric representation in *BP2* is an incomplete string description of polyphonic structures that can be processed by an efficient algorithm inferring a strict ordering of objects along symbolic time. For instance, given the information that a sequence of five sound-objects should be superimposed on another sequence of three objects, the algorithm would determine the following ordering of events:

(a b c d e, f g h)

a _ _ b _ _ c _ _ d _ _ e _ _
   f _ _ _ _ g _ _ _ _ h _ _ _ _

Incomplete representation
(polymetric expression)

Complete representation
(computed by algorithm)

The same algorithm is able to deal with multilayered polymetric expressions (*Interface*, 1990).

Sound-objects in *BP2* are sequences of elementary events, *i.e.*, messages to be dispatched to any sound processor. For instance, a conventional note is a simple sound-object represented as a note-on/note-off pair in the MIDI format. In addition, sound-objects may be assigned metrical and topological properties that determine their actual durations and locations in physical time. Durations are computed from the "local tempo" (assuming irregular beats in striated time, or no beat in smooth time) and from the metrical properties stipulating acceptable contraction/dilation ratios. Object locations are based on "time pivots" placed on "time streaks" (*i.e.*, beats). Topological properties introduce constraints on the overlapping and/or continuity of time intervals. Some objects need to be relocated or truncated until these constraints are fulfilled. In *BP2*, constraint-satisfaction is entirely handled by a fast algorithm (see Balaban *et al.*, 1991).

BP2 can be fully operated and synchronized by instructions received from its MIDI interface. It is possible to perform/repeat an item, modify tempo, reset rule weights, etc., using a MIDI keyboard and controllers, a MIDI sequencer or even another *BP2*. Real-time interaction is similar to the situation of several musicians improvising together while communicating information about parameters like tempo or compositional strategies through conventional (audible or inaudible) messages. A version of *BP2* running on Macintosh Classic is available as shareware. Registered users will receive upgraded versions and documentation.

REFERENCES

Bel, Bernard. "Bol Processor Grammars" and "Symbolic and Sonic Representations of Sound-Object Structures" in *Understanding Musical Activities: Readings in AI and Music*, ed. Mira Balaban, Kemal Ebcioğlu, and Otto Laske (Menlo Park, CA: AAAI Press, 1991).

Bel, Bernard. "Modelling Music with Grammars: Formal Language Representation in the *Bol Processor*," in *Computer Representations and Models in Music*, ed. Alan Marsden and Anthony Pople (London: Academic Press, forthcoming).

Bel, Bernard. "Time in Musical Structures," *Interface*, 19/2-3 (1990), 107-135.

Bernard Bel *is at the International Society for Traditional Arts Research, 62 rue Boudouresque, F-13007 Marseille, France; tel. +33 91-224256; fax 91-710808; e-mail: bel@frmop11.bitnet.*

Melody: Melodic Searching Software

Melody is a program by Spyros Gardikiotis to correlate one-part melodies and to classify them by style, scale, composer, place, and other criteria. The method of comparison involves the correlation of linear coefficients using G', a newly invented correlation method. The program can run external programs for input, editing, and output of data. Pitch and duration information may be defined by the user. Special routines evaluate intervals, relative durations, and relative durations of successive note pairs. The program runs on all fully compatible DOS machines.

REFERENCES

Gardikiotis, Spyros. "Πρόγραμμα H/Y για αρχειοθέτηση και συσχετισμό μουσικών κειμένων" ["Computer Program for Storing and Correlating Melodies"], Master's thesis, Aristoteles University of Thessaloniki, 1990.

Spyros Gardikiotis *created **Melody** as his Master's thesis project, under the direction of **Demetre Yannou**. Both may be reached at the School of Musical Studies, Aristoteles University of Thessaloniki, GR - 540 06 Thessaloniki, Greece.*

ASOUND: A Harmonic Analysis Program for MS DOS Machines

ASOUND is a program facilitating numerous harmonic operations on stored musical data [*cf. CM 1990*, pp. 116-7]. The program, developed in *Turbo Pascal* at the Czech Academy of Sciences by Maros Dudek on algorithms by Eva Ferková, runs in EGA mode on PC AT's (MS DOS 3.2 or higher). An interactive note editor for rapid input of notation is included, and audio playback is supported.

ASOUND recognizes 60 species of chords by their semitone structure. Provision for contextual (re)definition of chords in modulatory passages is made through the examination of user-designated musical sections and the possibility of suspending or changing the global key signature of the movement. Analytical results of chordal, tonal, and functional analysis can be displayed graphically. Test repertories contain works by Bach, Mozart, Kohler, Vanhal, Schubert, and Weber.

Continuing research focuses on the development of alternative means of input and creation of a compiler that would be compatible with ANSI standards.

Eva Ferková is at the Institute of Musicology SAV, Fajnorovo Nabrezie 7, 81364 Bratislava, Czechoslovakia; e-mail: ferko@mff.uniba.cs. She welcomes comments and queries and can provide a demonstration diskette to prospective users.

ELUS for Applications in FORTH

ELUS is a music applications development environment in FORTH. Running on MS-DOS and PS/2 machines and their compatibles, *ELUS* 1.0 extends the systems capabilities of FORTH-79 and -83 to enable programmers to concentrate on sound and graphics applications. The music component of *ELUS* includes a driver for the Roland MPU-401 MIDI interface, support for input and output from analog music systems via parallel communications (Modular Music Systems Digital Interface), compositional utilities for pitch and duration transformation, and serial, stochastic, and fractal operators.

ELUS software is available from Elusinian Enterprises, 7997 Phaeton Drive, Oakland, CA 94605-4212; tel. (415) 562-2055.

Interactive Multimedia in Higher Education:
The Goldsmith's College Project

As part of an experimental program funded by donations of hardware and software by IBM and a grant from the Leverhulme Trust, the Interactive Multimedia Music Education Group at Goldsmith's College set about evaluating the technical and pedagogical opportunities offered to the study of Music in Higher Education by emerging audio-visual computing. Technical evaluations were made of a range of multimedia software running under MS DOS on an IBM PS/2 model 80 with two CD-ROM readers, an optical scanner, and MIDI support. Software included *LinkWay* (from IBM), *Guide* 3.01 (from OWL), and *ToolBook* 1.5 (from Asymetrix) hypertext/hypermedia development systems.

Some courseware was created in order to demonstrate the new possibilities and to provide concrete examples of relevant materials to assist in the evaluation process. Some courseware was offered to students; other materials explored large-scale on-line text handling from the author's viewpoint.

The conclusions of the project point to the potential advantages and disadvantages of multimedia in music education. To summarize, it is felt that products and/or their applications at present emphasize passivity, while they should be engendering active approaches to information gathering and processing in support of creative thinking and the generation of new ideas. Future focus must be on providing increasingly sophisticated software tools for deeper interrogation of data rather than the industry-generated fashion for pretty pictures and anthropomorphized menus.

From our study it appears that the subject of music, if taken seriously, pushes expectations of multimedia systems well beyond the mere addition of sound to enticing graphic images. The project also demonstrates that it is viable to develop multimedia applications on the MS DOS platform, not merely on graphically oriented platforms such as those of the Macintosh and Atari.

David Burnand, who can be reached at the Music Department, Goldsmith's College, University of London, London SE14 6NW, England, can provide a full report on this project to interested readers.

Presto: A Program for Geometrical Composition

Presto is a composition tool for the Atari Mega ST4 showing tones as geometric points in 4-dimensional parameter-space (onset-time, pitch, duration, loudness) for each timbre. This geometrical data format may be translated into a standard MIDI-format. A composition may be produced by loading a standard MIDI or *Presto* file, by using *Presto* as a sequencer, or by drawing the notes with the mouse. The composition may be stored as standard MIDI or *Presto* file. *Presto* was developed to further the exploration of mathematical concepts, especially symmetries, in music theory.

Following the lemma of the mathematician Yoneda, *Presto* supports "perspective views." The editing of a composition is done on two different perspectives—that of the full score and that of the local (zoomed) score. One can perform complimentary operations, such as the inversion or transposition of pitches, on the score. In each of the six perspectives supported, all affine transformations may be applied to any part of the composition of the local score. One may define two-dimensional patterns, such as conjunctions between designated rhythmic patterns and pitch sequences, over a given motive. On the quadratic local score, any parameter-plane (duration/pitch etc.) may be selected.

Presto, which is written in *C*, is now being adapted for the Macintosh. A manual for the Atari version was published in 1990 by Marvin AG in Zurich. Research projects in music theory and neurobiology using *Presto* are running on Sun workstations.

REFERENCES

Mazzola, Guerino. *Geometrie der Töne.* Basel: Birkhäuser, 1990.

Mazzola, Guerino, and G. R. Hofmann. "Der Music Designer MDZ71 - Hard- und Software für die Mathematische Musiktheorie" in *Musik - Gehirn - Spiel: Beiträge zum IV. H. v. Karajan-Symposium*, ed. H. Petsche. Basel:Birkhäuser, 1989.

Mazzola, Guerrino, H. G. Wieser, F. Brunner, and D. Muzzulini, "A Symmetry-Oriented Mathematical Model of Counterpoint and Related Neurophysiological Investigations by Depth-EEG" in *Symmetry: Unifying Human Understanding*, II ed. I. Hargittai. New York: CAMWA/Pergamon Press, 1989.

Muzzulini, D. "Musical Modulation by Symmetries," Seminar für angewandte Mathematik, ETH Research Report No. 90-02, July 1990; forthcoming in the *Journal of Music Theory*.

*Presto has been developed by **Guerino Mazzola** and others under the auspices of the Projecktgruppe für Fundamentale Forschung in der Musik at the Eidgenossische Technische Hochschule in Zurich and the Arbeitsgruppe Graphische Datenverarbeitung of the Fraunhofer Gesellschaft in Darmstadt. Dr. Mazzola is at Wangenstrasse 11, 8600 Dübendorf, Switzerland; tel. +41 01-8219856; fax 01-8219851.*

Cognitive Approaches

Scientific Musicology as Cognitive Science

The aim of this enquiry is to provide a model, organized on methodological and epistemological grounds, of research in musicology. The key idea is to relate theoretical, psychological, and neurological research on music in the algorithmic framework developed by cognitive science (for an introduction to theories and mathematical concepts used in cognitive science (see Arbib 1987, 1989). While cognitive musicology is to be distinguished from musical informatics, these different areas of research are often strongly interconnected (Seifert 1990).

The goal of cognitive musicology is to develop theories of musical structure and musical processing which are empirically testable and are supported by research on music perception based on psychological and neurological facts. The best way to achieve this goal is to start with a formal description. The most developed theory today for this purpose is the generative theory of tonal music developed by Fred Lerdahl and Ray Jackendoff (1983). Since computer simulation plays an important role in cognitive science, a given theory or relevant parts of it should be implemented in a computer program. This program would therefore be a hypothesis about the basic structures and processes concerning music perception.

In cognitive psychology one speaks of the formal description of mental representations and processes. One may call all such formal descriptions schemata (Arbib 1989). The central conceptual link to relate the psychological idea of schemata with research on neurophysiological processing of higher brain functions, such as language understanding and music perception (see Marin 1989), is the module concept. On the computational side of the study of music perception, attention will be concentrated on the study of (1) parsing and (2) learning in parallel systems (Seifert 1991a, b).

To study parsing (1), one attempts to implement a mechanism which segments and classifies the perceptual data. Exploiting the idea of parallelism, the main task is to develop a concurrent parser. Helmut Schnelle's (1991) net-theoretical approach to concurrent parsing is used for implementation directly in electronic circuits. Since there exists an algorithm to transform context-free grammars via worksheets in a logical circuit, an important task will be to develop context-free descriptions of rhythmic, melodic, and harmonic structure at different levels and and in different musical systems to test these implementations.

(2) The problem of learning and/or induction (Seifert 1990) has been attacked by Bernard Bel (1990) in the special case of grammatical inference. Another strategy is to use production systems (used in music research by Jones *et al.*, 1990, in implementing the generative theory of Lerdahl and Jackendoff (1983) and genetic algorithms to realize classifier systems (Holland *et al.*, 1986) to exploit the ideas of competitive and cooperative computing in biological systems (Arbib 1989). An effort will be made to combine the approaches of net theory and schema theory.

REFERENCES

Arbib, Michael A. *Brains, Machines, and Mathematics*, 2nd edn. New York/Berlin: Springer Verlag, 1987.

Arbib, Michael A. *The Metaphorical Brain (Neural Networks and Beyond*, II). New York: Wiley, 1989.

Bel, Bernard. "Acquisition et représentation de connaissances en musique." Thesis, Aix-Marseille, 1990.

Jones, Jacqueline A., Don Scarborough, and Benjamin Miller. "GTSIM: A Computer Simulation of Music Perception" in the pre-print of the *Acts of the Conference "Music and Information Technology" MAI 90, 3-6 Octobre 1990* (Marseille, 1990), pp. 435-441.

Lerdahl, Fred, and Ray Jackendoff. *A Generative Theory of Tonal Music*. Cambridge, Mass.: MIT Press, 1983.

Marin, Oscar S. M. "Neuropsychology, Mental Cognitive Models, and Music Processing," *Contemporary Music Review*, 4 (1989), 255-263.

Seifert, Uwe. "Systematische Musiktheorie und Kognitionswissenschaft: Ein Beitrag zur Fundierung der Kognitiven Musikwissenschaft." Ph. D. Thesis, Hamburg University, 1990.

Seifert, Uwe. "Steps towards Computational Neuromusicology," Parts I and II, unpublished papers presented at the Musikwissenschaftliches Institut der Universität Hamburg, July 19 and 26, 1991. [1991a]

Seifert, Uwe. "The Schema Concept—A Critical Review of its Development and Current Use in Cognitive Science and Music Perception" in *Proceedings of the IX. Colloquium on Musical Informatics*, scheduled for publication in Genoa, December 1991. [1991b]

Schnelle, Helmut. *Die Natur der Sprache. Die Dynamik der Prozesse des Sprechens und Verstehens*. Berlin: de Gruyter, 1991.

Uwe Seifert can be reached c/o Prof. Dr. A. Schneider, Musikwissenschaftliches Institut der Universität Hamburg, Neue Rabenstrasse 13, W-2000 Hamburg 36, Germany; tel. +40 4123-2097; e-mail: FK00010@DHHUNI4.BITNET.

NeurSwing: A Connectionist Workbench for the Investigation of Swing in Afro-American Jazz

NeurSwing is a system of connectionist models, or neural nets, to investigate swing in Afro-American jazz by simulating the operation of a jazz rhythm section. From the harmonic grid of a tune, the system constructs a net which represents music data and plays in real time the lines of piano, bass, and drums. During the performance, the user can control the style of the rhythm section by turning three knobs—hot/cool, consonance/dissonance, as-is-ness/substitutions—that represent the input of a second, asynchronous net which determines the probabilities of harmonic, melodic, and rhythmic choices.

All substitution rules, rhythmic patterns, and drum figures, as well as the stylistic net, are external to the system, so that the expert system shell constituted by the nets can be configured alternatively in order to investigate the importance of some parameters for a particular kind of swing. In this sense, the system is a workbench for musicological study. In addition, with its present default rules, the system can be used as a didactical tool for jazz improvisation.

Denis L. Baggi is at the International Computer Science Institute in Lugano and can be reached at Casagrande 12, 6932 Breganzona, Switzerland; tel. +41 91-561578; fax 91-220409; e-mail: baggi@berkeley.edu. In 1991 he served as Visiting Professor at the University of California, Berkeley, and as guest editor of the July 1991 special music issue of **IEEE Computer**, which includes a fuller description of this project.

Cognitive Measures of Musical Phenomena

Quantification of music along cognitive parameters of perception and understanding is an efficient analytical process yielding data structures which lend themselves to processes of hierarchical analysis. This form of computer representation of musical knowledge is largely independent of the style of music involved and is therefore unspecialized or undifferentiated. The basic musical parameters of melody, harmony, texture, timbre, and rhythm may be subdivided into numerous cognitive subdomains. Melody, for example, may be examined for such properties as contour, duration, and consonance. Duration, texture, and timbre are properties that may be associated with harmony. Each of these properties may be treated as a vector within the cognitive musical space. The cognitive dimension of melody then becomes a multi-dimensional metric space which is, in turn, one of the metric spaces comprising the entire cognitive musical space. Each vector may be studied in isolation or combined in various ways with any other vector.

The quantification is essentially a distance function for a point in a metric space. Consonance is a distance function of the melodic pitch with respect to the root of the harmony with respect to the secondary key (if any) with respect to the primary key. Distance functions for melody can also be found in cognitive psychology studies and music theory. Studies and theories which provide a basis for the distance functions for harmony can be found in the fields of cognitive psychology and music theory.

These quantifying vectors can be shown to have useful properties which admit the application of computational theories and algorithms from other areas of computer science. Three such areas are computational geometry, language and compiler theory, and neural net algorithms. The vectorization of the cognitive music space yields a data representation which lends itself to currently popular theories of musical structure which have evolved from the original work of Heinrich Schenker.

Each event in a melody is defined as an M-tuple, where M is the number of cognitive subcomponents identified. The melody itself is a vector of M-tuples (organized in time), thus giving us an M-dimensional metric space. Each discrete harmonic event is defined as an H-tuple, where H is the number of cognitive subcomponents. Harmony is a vector of H-tuples, also organized in time, giving an H-dimensional metric space. Similarly, X-dimensional metric spaces may be constructed for other cognitive dimensions of music. Care should be taken to identify those dimensions which are dependent or interdependent for calculating values (*e.g.*, the dependence of melody upon harmony for its consonance values). Some consonance components may be combined in order to avoid inadvertently placing more weight on them than desired.

Each cognitive dimension is defined in light of the dichotomy between creation and resolution of tension, with the value associated with each discrete point in each dimension an expression of the dichotomy. A value of 1 may represent the maximum tension value, while 0 may represent the maximum relaxation, or stability, value.

Each vector may be viewed as the result of one phase of lexical analysis, with each set of values being the classification of a musical event according to the rules for that linguistic dimension. All vectors taken together then represent the entire "meaning" of the musical composition. Principles of linguistic reduction may easily be applied to vectors in isolation, in subgroups, or as a unit. These reductions in other linguistic-oriented applications usually yield some new insight or meaning into the object of analysis. These principles can be seen in relation to the first period of Chopin's Nocturne in Bb Minor (Figure 1).

Figure 1. Chopin: Nocturne in Bb Minor.

The high points are those of greater tension, the low points of greater stability. The reduction process revolves on the points of stability. The lowest reduction level (Figure 2) is derived from the linear combination of cognitive vectors. The horizontal axis represents time, while the vertical axis represents harmonic tension. Figures 3a and 3b indicate the tension-resolution contours for the next reduction level. The process may be continued until no points remain.

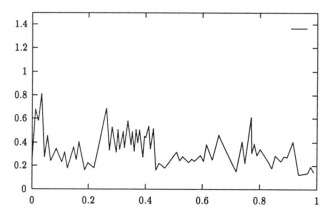

Figure 2. Reduction level 0. A tension-resolution contour, based on cognitive vectors, which becomes the basis for the next reduction level.

Figure 3a. Reduction level 1 indicated musically.

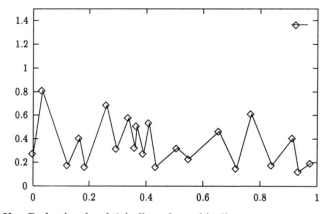

Figure 3b. Reduction level 1 indicated graphically.

This approach may be used as a foundation for more specialized tasks such as automated stylistic analysis, automated composition, and automated performance interpretation.

REFERENCES

Danner, Gregory. "The Use of Acoustic Measure of Dissonance to Characterize Pitch-class Sets, *Music Perception*, 3/1 (1985), 103-122.

Deutsch, Diana, and John Feroe.   "The Internal Representation of Pitch Sequences in Tonal Music," *Psychological Review*, 88/6 (1981), 503-522.

Dowling, W. Jay. "Scale and Contour: Two Components of a Theory of Memory for Melodies," *Psychological Review*, 85/4 (1978), 341-354.

Hindemith, Paul. *The Craft of Musical Composition*. London: Schott and Co., Ltd., 1942.

Jones, M.R. "Dynamic Pattern Structure in Music: Recent Theory and Research," *Perception and Psychophysics*, 41/6 (1987), 621-634.

Krumhansl, Carol, and Edward Kessler.   "Tracing the Dynamic Changes in Perceived Tonal Organization in a Spatial Representation of Musical Keys," *Psychological Review*, 89/4 (1982), 334-368.

Schenker, Heinrich. *Free Composition*, tr. Ernst Oster. New York: Longman, 1935.

Sloboda, John. *The Musical Mind: The Cognitive Psychology of Music*.   Oxford: Clarendon Press, 1985.

Larry Albright is in the Department of Computer Science, Box 41771, University of Southwestern Louisiana, Lafayette, LA 70501; tel. (318) 231-6638; e-mail: albright@gator.cacs.usl.edu.

Feature-Extraction Processes in Musical Pattern Recognition

Artificial neural networks are collections of neuron-like elements connected much like real neurons in the brain, but much simpler in their structure and operation. The elements form discrete layers with connections between, and sometimes within, layers. The weight on connections between elements can be modified, and it is this facility which allows a network to "learn."   Given a pattern representing a particular musical composition and a learning rule, the network can be programmed to alter its connection strengths so that it always gives the same output to the particular composition. In many instances, these models are said to embody cognitive processes characteristic of human listeners. The aim of this study is to seek evidence for the psychological reality of the recognition processes embodied in connectionist models of music recognition.

The study involves three major stages: (1) the identification of local and global features of tonal music which are thought to be extracted by listeners in music recognition tasks; (2) the experimental investigation of whether the specified features are used by musically trained and untrained listeners; and (3) the simulation of feature-extraction and feature-weighting processes in a connectionist model of music recognition.

Features characteristic of western tonal music were derived from a two-dimensional matrix wherein music was represented as a series of frequencies plotted over time. Local features derived from the matrix were interval magnitude, direction of pitch change, and closure; global features included melodic contour, tonality, transposition, tempo, and rhythm. Visual pattern-recognition theory provided a framework for the design of the experiments and a theoretical basis for the experimental hypotheses. According to this theory, if a feature is used in recognition, then manipulation of that feature should affect recognition.

In experimentation, local features were tested using a discrimination task where short musical compositions (four to eight bars) were played in pairs. Subjects judged whether the second composition in the pair was the same or different from the first (where the first was always the "standard" composition). In fifty percent of the trials the second composition was modified so that it contained manipulation of the feature under investigation. In the experiment investigating melodic contour, for example, Class-1 compositions were characterized by a smooth contour, while Class-2 compositions were characterized by a jagged contour. In the six experiments completed to date, recognition performance of trained subjects has been significantly better than that of untrained subjects. Both musically trained and untrained listeners have been able to discriminate between, or classify compositions by attending to a particular feature. Hence evidence has been obtained for feature-extraction processes mediating music recognition.

The musical stimuli and instructions were presented on a Macintosh SE computer and responses made by the subject were recorded by the computer. Compositions were stored as data files and read by a program written in Microsoft *QuickBASIC*. An external timer was used to record reaction time as the internal Macintosh timer was found to be unreliable when the sound generator was in use (see Kieley and Higgins, 1989). The classification task which was used to investigate melodic contour has been simulated using the *MacBrain* software package. Simulation of the discrimination task has been achieved using a simple two-layer perceptron. The perceptron has been programmed to discriminate modified compositions from the standard, where the modified compositions contained the manipulated interval magnitude feature. A major disadvantage of many connectionist models of music (*e.g.*, Rumelhart and McClelland, 1986; Linster, 1989) is that the input layer presents all the frequency values in parallel, rather than in a sequential manner characteristic of actual music recognition tasks.

Work continues on refining sequential input to the connectionist model and the inclusion of masking and decay rates to simulate the physiological constraints within auditory tasks. The salience or weighting of local and global features of music within various contexts is also being investigated.

REFERENCES

Bharucha, J. "Music Cognition and Perceptual Facilitation: A Connectionist Framework," *Music Perception*, 5 (1987), 1-30.

Gjerdingen, R. O. "Categorization of Musical Patterns by Self-organizing Neuronlike Networks," *Music Perception*, 7 (1990), 339-370.

Kieley, J. M. and Higgins, T. S. (1989). "Precision Timing Options for the Apple Macintosh," *Behavior Research Methods, Instruments, and Computers*, 21 (1989), 259-264.

Leman, Marc. "Sequential Musical Information Processing with PDP-Networks," *Proceedings of the First Workshop on AI and Music, Minneapolis/St. Paul, AAAI-88*, (Menlo Park, CA: AAAI, 1989), 163-172.

Linster, C. "Rhythm Analysis with Back-propagation" in *Connectionism in Perspective*, ed. R. Pfeifer, Z. Schreter, F. Fogelman-Soulie, and L. Steels. North-Holland: Elsevier, 1989.

Marsden, Alan, and Anthony Pople. "Towards a Connected Distributed Model of Musical Listening," *Interface*, 18 (1989), 61-72.

Rumelhard, D.E., and J. L. McClelland. *Parallel Distributed Processing: Explorations in the Microstructure of Cognition*. Vols. I and II. Cambridge, MA: MIT Press, 1986.

Todd, P.M., and D. G. Loy, (eds.). *Music and Connectionism*. Cambridge, MA: MIT Press, 1991.

Catherine Stevens is in the Department of Psychology at the University of Sydney, Sydney, New South Wales 2006, Australia; tel. +61 2-692-3227; fax 2-692-2603; e-mail: kates@psychvax.psych.su.oz. She is willing to provide additional details on experimental design, results, and computer programs.

Fractal Approaches to Analysis and Composition

Fractal geometry is a recent field of mathematics founded on the work of the Polish mathematician Benoit Mandelbrot. There are several branches within the field, which has gained particular currency in the past five years for its synthetic applications in computer graphics. The concept of fractal images has been explored particularly in the study of nature, and many commentaries perceive fractals to be at work in fern leaves, snowflakes, clouds, and coastlines. In music, fractal paradigms are being used in both analysis and composition. Because the subject is unfamiliar to many of our readers, we have attempted to provide both a brief introduction to the subject and a brief summary of recent work in the field before proceeding to contributed articles.

A popular branch of study explores the observation that the magnitude of a phenomenon is inversely related to the frequency of its occurrence. This is often referred to as the Zipf-Mandelbrot law. According to this law, the frequency of an occurrence is equal to a constant divided by the magnitude raised to a constant power α (α is most often in the range 1 to 2). This law can be applied to musical analysis in a variety of ways, with results that will differ according to the particular musical parameters evaluated as well as the quantity of data examined, and the quality of its representation. Frequency studies of both static parameters, such as pitch and duration, and dynamic ones, such as pitch change (*i.e.*, intervals) and volume change, have been undertaken.

Fractals are created by the process known as recursive subdivision or midpoint displacement. Mandelbrot traces the midpoint displacement procedure to Archimedes (who used it to evaluate the area between a parabola and a chord) and regards it as the "first documented step towards calculus" (Pietgen and Saupe, p. 11). A regular scheme of recursive subdivision at the midpoint may be seen in the series of images shown on the following page. The recursive image (*e.g.*, the Sierpinsky triangle used in Illustration 1) consistently displaces the midpoint of a line or curve in the original image. The relationship of common shapes repeated over a range of scales is called one of self-similarity.

The constancy of the general shape may be less easily recognized when randomization is combined with midpoint displacement. This process is represented by the non-equivalent triangles in Illustration 2. The leap from computer-generated images mimicking natural phenomena, such as the fractal "mountain" in Illustration 2, to actual natural phenomena, such as the close-up of a shoreline cliff shown in Illustration 3, admits further randomization to the process.

Illustrations by courtesy of Michael McGuire.

Illustration 1. Midpoint displacement with self-similar images.

Illustrations by courtesy of Michael McGuire.

Illustration 2. Midpoint displacement with randomized images.

Photograph by courtesy of Michael McGuire.

Illustration 3. Cliffs at Salt Point, Mendocino Coast, California (detail).

One can imagine the lines of the triangle being replaced by spans of time, which may be subdivided in a recursive manner. Musical events or attributes could then be attached to these points in time. Analogues to the reciprocity between order and randomness expressed in the fractal mountain have been sought, using acoustical data, in the temporal realm by Richard Voss and others. Working with acoustical data in the Seventies, Voss and Clark found a fractal dimension in volume (amplitude) but not in pitch (frequency). These studies have been taken as a challenge by other researchers.

One needs to be cautious about evaluating the success of any "fractal type" analysis. Where F = frequency, K = a constant, and M = magnitude, the fractal formula $F = K/M^{\alpha}$ is quite general and can be made approximately to match almost any phenomenon which has the property that the further one parameter goes toward an extreme (of pitch, duration, etc.), the fewer instances will be found.

While the mechanics of the analysis attract considerable interest, the occurrence of such distributions does not necessarily mean that the phenomenon rigorously follows the fractal law. Although randomization of detail may be an asset in composition, it can provide an excuse for vagueness in analysis and "poor fits" in results. Data selectivity, for example in *1/f* (or 1/*M*) analyses used to express the scaling of randomness in time, offers scope for "proving" the existence of general laws by tailoring the sample to the hypothesis. Yet by requiring the compilation of frequency tables for many parameters, the exploration of the possibility of a fractal dimension in musical works could have important if incidental consequences for other quantitative approaches to musical analysis.

In recent work, Moisei Boroda, whose study (1984) is too long to reproduce here, has explored the Zipf-Mandelbrot equation as applied to the repetitions of musical segments in both classical music of recent centuries and folk songs from Georgia and Armenia. His segments typically consist of one to five notes; occasionally one note belongs to two adjacent segments. After computing the number of segments occurring once, twice, and so forth, he attempted to show that these works follow a form of the Zipf-Mandelbrot law. Among his findings was that the theoretical plot was followed more closely when complete compositions, as opposed to excerpts, were tested. However, he was dissatisfied with the quality of agreement. As a consequence, Boroda attempted to simplify his study and improve its statistics by considering only the rhythmic nature of his segments.

The contribution of the Hsüs, consisting of two recently published articles, is supplemented in the short piece printed below. In their study of self-similarity (1990) they seek to relate the Zipf-Mandelbrot equation to different kinds of music, ranging from Bach inventions to Swiss children's songs. They postulate that the melodic line is not fractal, but the succession of intervals within it may be. Their publications consider the number of occurrences of different melodic intervals throughout a work (intervallic directions, up or down, are not differentiated). Typically they find that intervals of 2 to 5 half-steps may fall within a factor of 2 of a Zipf-Mandelbrot line. They discuss differences in the Zipf-Mandelbrot parameter α for diverse compositions.

A separate approach to the parameterization of music (1991) tests the property of linear fractals to retain their degree of complexity when "viewed" with the same ratio of resolution to width of view—self-similarity independent of scale. They changed "scale" and "resolution" by systematic elimination of notes from the works under consideration. In a series of reductions, they retained every second note, then every third, and so forth (see the example on p. 99) to the point where only three notes remained in Bach's Invention in C Major. The resulting compressed "works" were judged through listening to retain a resemblance the music of Bach. They claim similar results for music by Mozart.

Algorithmic composers have found in fractals a rich field of exploration. Images may be augmented, diminished, rotated, and subjected to many other transformations. Janet Thomas has, among other things, used the Zipf-Mandelbrot distribution, with $\alpha = 1$, to generate sequential notes. Her contention is that geometrical principles of nature and music are directly related and that thus the Zipf-Mandelbrot distribution is applicable to music, whereas simple random choice of pitches and durations is not. The choice of $\alpha = 1$ follows from her belief that the brain's response to stimuli follows such a formula. Consequently, the $\alpha = 1$ music has a feeling of balance and proportion. These ideas are elaborated below.

REFERENCES

Boroda, Moisei. "The Organization of Repetitions in the Musical Composition: Towards a Quantitative-Systematic Approach" [originally published in Estonian and Russian in Tartu, Estonia, in 1984], *Musikometrika*, 2 (1990), 53-105.

Gardner, Martin. "White and Brown Music, Fractal Curves, and 1/f Noise," *Scientific American* (April 1978), 16ff.

Mandelbrot, Benoit. *Fractals: Form, Chance, Dimension*, tr. by the author from *Les objets fractals* (Paris, 1975). San Francisco: W. W. Freeman, 1977.

Mandelbrot, Benoit. *The Fractal Geometry of Nature*. New York: W. W. Freeman, 1982.

Pietgen, Heinz-Otto, and Dietmar Saupe (eds.). *The Science of Fractal Images*. New York: Spring-Verlag, 1988.

Voss, Richard F. "1/f Noise in Music: Music from 1/f Noise," *Journal of the Acoustical Society of America*, 63 (1978), 258-63.

Voss, Richard F., and J. Clarke. "'1/f Noise' in Music and Speech," *Nature*, 258 (1975), 317-8.

The editors wish to acknowledge the assistance of **Michael McGuire**, *the author of* **An Eye for Fractals: A Graphic and Photographic Essay** *(Redwood City, CA: Addison-Wesley, 1991; ISBN 0-201-55440-2), in making available the illustrations and of* **Clive Field**, *a physicist at the Stanford Linear Accelerator Center, Stanford, CA 94309, in preparing the preceding commentary.*

Self-Similarity in Music

We have been engaged in verifying fractal geometry and exploring the implication of self-similarity of music. We hold that classical music, such as Bach's inventions, has a scale-independence which can be compressed on a scale of 1/2, 1/3, 1/4, 1/8, and so forth. We have found that fundamental patterns persist in fractal compression after 1/2, 2/3, 3/4, 7/8, etc. of the notes are removed. An abstract of music serves the purpose of summarizing its themes just as the abstract of a scientific paper summarizes its content.

The algorithms of our program involve these operations:

1. Assign a code j to each musical note, which is defined on the basis of its acoustic frequency, or pitch (f) relative to a standard pitch (f_o), and by the relation

$$f/f_o = (2)^{j/12}$$

2. Resolve each coded note with a beat L (full, half, quarter, 1/8th, etc.) into n-number of notes of the shortest beat S (commonly a sixteenth in Bach and a thirty-second in more modern music) where

$$n = L/S$$

A half note, for example, would be converted to eight sixteenth notes.

3. Select every other (for 1/2 reduction), or every third (for 1/3 reduction), or every fourth (for 1/4 reduction) coded note, and eliminate all other notes.

4. Recombine the resolved notes into a whole. Eight sixteenth notes, having been reduced to four sixteenth notes during a half-reduction, are now recombined to make one quarter note.

To transform the audio input into visual signals, we have digitized the pitches. These are plotted against the successive [event] numbers of notes in the composition. Our computer printout gives the musical composition, now reduced, in coded notes, and we work manually to translate that into conventional music.

The application of this methodology is to find the essence of a new kind of structural essence for each composition. We realize that analyses of many compositions are needed before one can begin to find the rules of mathematical structuring of music. We expect,

Start of Bach's Two-Part Invention in C Major, BWV 772.

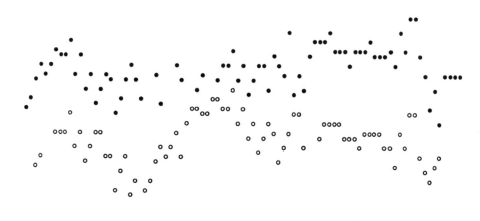

Second-order reduction of the complete C-Major Invention.

The black dots represent the right hand part, and the white ones the left.

nevertheless, that great music should show a structure like a great edifice. Also, we suggest that we could gain insight into the structuring of classical music, such as Bach's, by the use of the so-called mid-point enhancement technique. We have, however, not learned this technique, and would welcome communications for possible cooperative research.

REFERENCES

Hsü, Kenneth J., and Andrew J. Hsü. "Fractal Geometry of Music: The Physics of Melody," *Proceedings of the National Academy of Sciences, USA*, 87 (1990), 938-41.

Hsü, Kenneth J., and Andrew J. Hsü. "Self-Similarity of the '1/f noise' Called Music," forthcoming in *Proceedings of the National Academy of Sciences, USA*, 88 (1991).

Kenneth Hsü *is a geologist at the Eidgenössische Technische Hochschule, Zurich. His son* **Andrew Hsü** *is at the Konservatorium und Musikhochschule, Zurich. They describe themselves as beginners in programming and would appreciate responses from readers to help them improve their program and to devise a program to translate their coded music into a musical score. They can be reached at Frohburgstrasse 96, 8006 Zurich, Switzerland; tel. +41 1-3621462; fax 1-252-7008.*

Fractals in Algorithmic Composition

Natural models have always lent inspiration to composers, albeit until the present day purely of a semantic kind. The models of nature found in fractals lend inspiration for a novel syntactic function to parallel the semantic. In an attempt to explore the relationship between the fractal forms and textures in nature and the generation of musical form and texture, several types of fractal generation—from the Koch curve model of recursive algorithm to the statistical self-similarity models of fractional noises, in particular 1/f—have been implemented. The processes involving 1/f do not usually produce memorable themes as such, but they work particularly well at high speeds over long time spans, in which the statistically self-similar shapes become more "comprehensible" through repetition, yet avoid the result of tedium by not being mere reiterations of a stochastic "theme." The result is a music generally regarded as accessible, interesting, pleasant, and containing a balance of predictability and unpredictability.

In composition the most chaotic sequences exhibit fractal patterning, resulting as they do from endless sequences of bifurcation. These sequences can easily be mapped onto musical parameters capable of quantification—*e.g.* frequency (pitch), intensity (amplitude), and duration—and subsequently used as material in a piece. There are many other ways of interpreting the output of a chaotic system. A particularly fruitful approach lies in the utilization of the periodicity/aperiodicity fluctuation scheme, which mirrors the equilibrium/tension (disturbance) flow in many traditional musics. Another of my chaos algorithms utilizes different output values as pointers to different events: timbre-changes, chord-changes, and so on, to build up structures both unpredictable yet non-random.

The programs exhibiting the methods described here are written in the *C* and *Lisp* programming languages and output the musical results via MIDI. They run on the Atari ST. The programs are aimed at a user working in the electro-acoustic composition environment, and thus consist of user-interactive interfaces to specify input of parameter values and effect parameter-value changes during output.

REFERENCES

Thomas, Janet. "Fractals in Algorithmic Composition with Computers," *Computers in Music Research Conference Handbook* (Belfast: The Queen's University, 1991), pp. 12-3.

Janet Thomas is completing a M.Sc. in Music Technology at the University of York, England; e-mail: JPT4@VAXA.YORK.AC.UK.AC. She welcomes contact with others engaged in the exploration of fractals in music.

Visual Music:
Commercial Software for Exploring Fractals

Dual-Medium Fractals

In one program by Hugh McDowell, a selected area of the screen provides the basis for musical generation. In another, fractal images and music are created simultaneously by a common algorithm. Both are available from CFM, 121 Ferrestone Road, Hornsey, London N8X 7BX, England.

Fractal Music

Chris Sansom's *Fractal Music* for the Atari ST utilizes user-selected starting numbers to generate music for as many as 16 MIDI voices. Enquiries may be addressed to the composer at 4 Sharon St., Alexandra Grove, London N12 8NX, England.

FracTunes

For the IBM PC, Bourbaki Inc., PO Box 2867, Boise, ID 83701; tel. (800) 289-1347, offers *FracTunes*, which animates *PCX* graphics image files. Images may be animated either by MIDI performance or by stored music files.

Systems for the Visually Impaired

Efforts to use computers to improve access by the visually impaired to musical information extend back a decade or more. A number of the developers of notational software who regularly contribute to this publication used their systems early on to create large-print editions of music. The idea of generating scores in Braille seemed like a natural alternative use of encoded information, and many systems we have reported on in earlier issues have expressed an interest in this area.

When we reported on some current efforts to generate Braille notation in the 1989 issue of *CM* (p. 25), we became aware of the fact that while Braille music notation is, in a sense, a code for music that is older than any of those currently in use in music software, it exists in a great many (predominantly national) dialects. Visually impaired readers tell us that these dialects are not entirely stable.

They also tell us that their interests lie not so much in producing notation in Braille as in producing common notation of arrangements and compositions for the use of sighted musicians and in generating MIDI performances to facilitate learning new music by ear. Some of these needs are addressed in this year's reports.

Tokyo: A Bilateral Translation System between Printed Music and Braille

It is not always easy for blind people to obtain Braille musical scores, because Braille musical production requires a knowledge of music, Braille, and Braille musical notation [of which there are many dialects]. The automated bilateral translation system between printed music and Braille developed in our laboratory over the past several years has the capability of converting almost all symbols in a piano score into Braille within seconds and embossing them with a Braille-writer automatically.

User's requests during the above-mentioned testing led us to develop an inverse translation system (c) that converts a Braille music score back to a printed score for use with a desk-top computer. Besides being useful for translating a Braille musical score created by a blind person into a printed music score automatically, this system is also useful for checking the results of the printed-music-to-Braille translation.

(a) Original score.

(b) A Braille transcription of the same music.

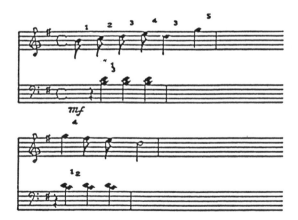

(c) A translation from Braille to printed music.

Recently, the printed-music-to-Braille translation system has been rearranged and simplified using a desk-top computer, which can be used without special equipment and by any person, not just by music experts and Braille music and computer specialists. A test score is limited in score size and in the range of fonts used for music symbols. For information representing printed music, two kinds of data are available: one is the data previously obtained by the automatic music-score reading device in our laboratory, and the other is the data directly obtained by the user with a commercially available manual music processor. The system has two outputs, one for a Braille-writer and the other for a sound board or a MIDI instrument. It is now being subjected to practical testing in several schools for the blind and rehabilitation centers in Tokyo and Osaka.

Besides being useful for translating a Braille musical score created by a blind person into a printed music score automatically, this system is also useful for checking the results of the printed-music-to-Braille translation.

REFERENCES

Proceedings of the International Workshop on Computer Applications for the Visually Handicapped (1990-1), forthcoming.

Sadamu Ohteru's *laboratory is located in the Department of Applied Physics, Waseda University, 3-4-1 Okubo, Shinjuku-ku, Tokyo 169, Japan; tel. 81 3-203-4141, fax 3-200-2567; sohteru@jpnwas00.ac.jp.*

Toulouse: Braille Music Transcription and Analysis

Ongoing research at the Centre Tobia in Toulouse is intended to create an environment in which blind musicians can work with sighted musicians. Initially a transcription program to produce scores in French or American Braille notation was devised. This program is currently being expanded to include a broader spectrum of musical information and to support the creation of conventional printed scores.

As a second phase, we have devised a program to teach harmony. It includes a document-creation module and a help module. For the document-creation module, a speech synthesizer facilitates verbal input and editing through the use of an aural question/answer format. The input document is automatically coded on a linear form and is then analyzed and stored. The intermediate code is an alphanumerical one.

The help module guides the student during the learning period and may be used by the teacher to test the competence and scope of the software. An expert system is used to analyze answers given by students.

Since no standard for music representation currently exists, interfaces for various sound and printing systems are being developed.

REFERENCES

Baptiste, Nadine. "Un système d'apprentissage assisté par ordinateur pour l'harmonie musicale pouvant être utilisé par des non voyants." Thesis, Paul Sabatier University, 1990.

Baptiste, Nadine, and Monique Truquet. "La Musique assistée par ordinateur: système d'enseignement assisté par ordinateur de l'harmonie," Proceedings of the Fourth *Salon International de l'Informatique, de la Télématique, des Equipments de Bureau et de la Bureautique, Casablanca, October 1989.*

Baptiste, Nadine, and Monique Truquet. "Harmony Program Learning for the Blind Person," proceedings of the *Sixth International Workshop on Computer Applications for the Visually Handicapped, Leuven [Belgium], 19-21 Septembre 1990.*

Baptiste, Nadine, and Monique Truquet. "How to Help Visually Impaired Musicians: Automatic Braille Transcription," forthcoming in the Proceedings of the *First International Conference on Information Technology, Computerization, and Electronics in the Workplace for People with Disabilities, Washington, DC, December 1991.*

Frontin, J. "Un système interactif de transcription de partitions musicales universelles pour non voyants." Thesis, Paul Sabatier University, 1981.

Nadine Baptiste and Monique Truquet are at the Centre Tobia, Université Paul Sabatier, 118, route de Narbone, 31062 Toulouse Cedex, France; tel. +33 61-55-69-44; fax 61-55-64-70.

Florence: An MS DOS Environment for the Visually Impaired

Work-in-progress at the Florence Conservatory is part of the Concerted Action on Technology and Blindness, a research program sponsored by European Economic Community. The main applications are directed toward:

(1) Braille transcription of printed music. Here new programs help the user to encode a musical score alphanumerically and then to print a Braille edition.

(2) Automated printing of a conventional musical score. The fact that many commercial notation programs use a graphic interface renders them unsuitable for the visually impaired. We are exploring new interfaces to generate conventional printed notation. The goal is to allow the blind musician to prepare and print a score without the need of a copyist.

(3) Musical education. New interfaces to simplify the learning of music by the visually impaired are being explored.

(4) Use of a voice synthesizer with commercial programs. It is possible to use a voice synthesizer to read all the commands listed on the screen with those programs (*e.g.*, *SCORE*) that do not use a graphical user interface. In this context the user can hear data input from the computer keyboard.

The starting point of our own plan for a workstation that can be used by both sighted and visually impaired musicians is *TELETAU*, a mainframe-based software package whose user interface is completely text-oriented. *TELETAU* provides for (1) music encoding, (2) algorithmic composition, (3) musical data processing, (4) handling of encoded works stored in a machine-readable library, (5) musical education, and (6) music analysis. We are currently in the process of conversion to the MS DOS environment. At present the system can perform several operations of the *TELETAU* system in the areas of encoding and management of previously encoded pieces. We use *Adagio* software and a standard MIDI interface for sound output.

REFERENCES

Nencini, G., P. Grossi, G. Bertini, L. Camilleri, and L. Tarabella. "*TELETAU:*—A Computer Music Permanent Service" in the *Proceedings of the International Computer Music Conference 1986*. San Francisco: Computer Music Association, 1986.

Lelio Camilleri, Francesco Giomi, and P. Graziani are at the Divisione Musicologica CNUCE/C.N.R. and the Conservatorio di Musica "L.Cherubini", Piazza delle Belle Arti 2, 50122 Firenze, Italy; tel: +39 55-282105; e-mail: CONSERVA@IFIIDG.Bitnet. L. Taggi is at the Istituto di Ricerca sulle Onde Elettromagnetiche del C.N.R., Via Panciatichi 64, 50127 Firenze, Italy; tel: +39 55-4378512.

Automatic Recognition and Related Topics

Experiments in the recognition of musical notation, which depend on spacial interpretation, can be traced back more than two decades. *CM* reported on them in *1990*, pp. 36-45, in *1989*, pp. 31-4, and in *1988*, pp. 38-40. They continue to be numerous and vigorously pursued, as this year's contributions show. Readers may also want to follow the work of William McGee and Paul Merkley, reported in *CM* last year (pp. 42-3), which is now fully described in "The Optical Scanning of Medieval Music," *Computers and the Humanities*, 25/1 (1991), 47-53.

This year we also include reports on experiments concerned with automatic recognition of performed music and of musical gesture, which depend on the interpretation of various durational and rhythmic properties of performance, often in addition to other factors. We begin with reports on the automatic recognition of musical notation.

Cardiff: University of Wales

The aim of the present study, initiated in 1987 at the College of Cardiff, University of Wales, is the production of a low-cost system allowing automatic computer entry of musical data for music databases, music editing, and music printing. Its repertory is mainly concerned with printed music notation, provided that the notation in use is fairly common. However, the system has also been tested on some neat handwritten notation, which was successfully recognized, but the recognition methods are fairly reliant on the proportion of music symbols following the conventions of printed music, so it is not anticipated that the majority of handwritten music could be read by this method. The work is being undertaken for a Ph.D. thesis in the Department of Computing Mathematics.

The main development this year is the inclusion of some music syntax checking, to check the validity of the output of the system. The intention of this is to help an operator correct the output data. It is our belief that it will be very difficult for any system to be 100% accurate in the immediate future, for various reasons. While it is important that a recognition system should be able successfully to identify as much of the notation as possible, some "errors of rejection" are inevitable, and a current priority is for a system to identify all the possible errors in order to make it as simple as possible for a human operator to correct the output.

REFERENCES

Clarke, Alastair, Malcolm Brown, and Mike Thorne. "Problems to be faced by the Developers of Computer Based Automatic Music Recognisers," *Proceedings of the International Computer Music Conference 1990* (San Francisco: Computer Music Association, 1990), pp. 345-347.

Alastair Clarke *is a Tutorial Research Fellow in the Department of Computing Mathematics at the University of Wales, College of Cardiff, P.O. Box 916, Cardiff CF2 4YN, United Kingdom; tel. +44 0222-874000 X5519; fax 666182; e-mail: alastair@uk.ac.cf.cm.* [CM inadvertently neglected to attach Alastair Clarke's name to the description of his work in last year's issue, on p. 38, and offers its belated apologies.]

Guildford: University of Surrey

The research on optical recognition of music that has been in progress for several years [see *CM 1990*, pp. 36-45, and *1988*, pp. 38-40] is now being ported from the 80386-based Sun 386i, which we were originally using, onto a SPARCstation 2. This move has been occasioned by the success of our submission under Sun Microsystems' Academic Equipment Grant Scheme, which also will provide a SPARCstation SLC, a 669MB hard disk, a laser printer, a CD-ROM drive, and a tape drive.

The music recognition software is now in place; some porting of utilities remains to be completed. The flat-bed scanner will be interfaced with a PC which will in turn be networked to the workstations.

The work reported last year can be illustrated with an excerpt from the work of C. P. E. Bach, shown in the new edition by Oxford University Press and in a scanned version output in *SCORE*.

C. P. E. Bach: Sonata No. 131 in E Minor.

C. P. E. Bach: printed output, via SCORE, from scanned information.

More recently we have attempted to process early printed music, starting with madrigals from the early seventeenth century. [The quality of the original image shown on the next page is poor because it is reproduced from a photocopy of a fax of a photocopy.]

Original material: Giovan Domenico Montella, the *Basso* part of "Dolce primavera"
from *Il settimo libro de madrigali e cinque voci* (Naples, 1605).

The processed output shows (1) removal of the large graphic at top left and some lines
(shadows) at the top and left of the image; (2) identification and extraction of the text
underlay; (3) identification of staff lines; and (4) isolation of musical symbols (shaded
regions) ready for recognition. The code to achieve recognition of the isolated symbols
is now being written.

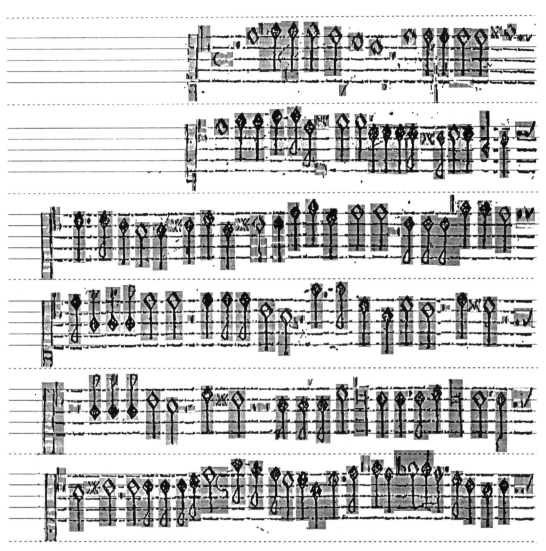

Processed output: Montella's "Dolce primavera."

REFERENCES

Carter, N. P., and R. A. Bacon. "Automatic Recognition of Printed Music" in *Structured Document Image Analysis*, ed. H. S. Baird, H. Bunke, and K. Yamamoto (Heidelberg: Springer-Verlag, Sept. 1991).

Nicholas P. Carter is in the Depts. of Music and Physics, University of Surrey, Guildford, Surrey GU2 5XH, England; tel. +44 0483-571281, X3049; fax 300803; e-mail: npc@ph.surrey.ac.uk.

Montréal: McGill University

In research leading to a master's thesis at McGill University, Ichiro Fujinaga used a series of projections to capture data elements in monophonic works and single parts of polyphonic ones. Among the steps in the process he developed were these:

1. Locate the system by creating a Y [vertical] projection of the entire page onto the vertical axis.

2. Analyze the system.

  a. Locate the staff with a series of Y projections.

  b. Locate individual symbols by taking an X [horizontal] projection of the entire staff.

  c. Segment each symbol by establishing its vertical boundaries and then taking an X projection of the redefined rectangle.

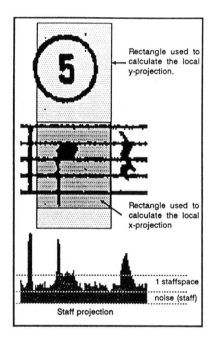

Rectangle used to calculate the local y-projection.

Rectangle used to calculate the local x-projection

1 staffspace

noise (staff)

Staff projection

The rates of accuracy for both pitch and duration of all elements encountered in four sets of samples scanned ranged from 64% to 82%. The scanner used was a Datacopy 710 (200 d.p.i.). The programs were written in Microsoft C 4.0 and 5.0 on a PC. On average it took 30 seconds to scan a page and 15 seconds to process the information.

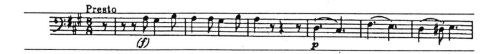

The McGill System.

BASS CLEF
3 SHARP(S)
UP WHITE SPACE 4
EIGHTH REST
BAR LINE
EIGHTH REST
EIGHTH REST
FLAG_DN 1 LINE 1
DN BLACK SPACE 1
DN BLACK SPACE 0
BAR LINE
DN BLACK LINE 1
FLAG_DN 1 LINE 1
DN BLACK SPACE 1
DN BLACK SPACE 0
BAR LINE
DN BLACK LINE 1
EIGHTH REST
Q_REST
EIGHTH REST
BAR LINE
DN BLACK LINE 3
SHARP/NAT
BAR LINE
DN BLACK LINE 2
DOT
DN BLACK SPACE 2
DOT
BAR LINE
DN BLACK LINE 3
SHARP/NAT
DN BLACK LINE 3
DN BLACK SPACE 2
DOT
BAR LINE

This page: Sample [from the cello part of Haydn's quartet Op. 9, No. 6] showing the frame in which the first staff is located [above] and the file produced [at left].

Preceding page: definition of staff and symbol space.

REFERENCES

Fujinaga, Ichiro. "Optical Music Recognition using Projections." Master's thesis, McGill University, 1988.

Fujinaga, Ichiro, Bo Alphonce, and Bruce Pennycook. "Issues in the Design of an Optical Music Recognition System," *Proceedings of the International Computer Music Conference 1989* (San Francsico: CMA, 1989), 113-6.

Fujinaga, Ichiro, Bo Alphonce, Bruce Pennycook and Natalie Boisvert. "Optical Recognition of Musical Notation by Computer," *Computers in Music Research* I (1989).

Pennycook, Bruce, "Towards Advanced Optical Music Recognition," *Advanced Imaging* (April, 1990).

Ichiro Fujinaga is continuing his research at McGill University, 3459 McTavish Street, Montréal, PQ H3A 1Y1, Canada.

Tokyo: Computerized Dance-Step Recognition and Musical Accompaniment

Music and dance have been closely related since ancient times. Music has created new dances and dances have produced new music. In the field of computer music, the link between music and human body movement is not yet very strong. We are engaged in research to create a dance accompaniment system named "MAI" (the name of an old Japanese style of dance). It is designed to recognize a dance pattern in real time and to generate appropriate dance music by selecting a score from a previously stored database of musical works.

A pair of dancers on the stage starts dancing, for example, a waltz without music. As shown in the illustration, a high resolution CCD video camera attached to the ceiling follows the white silk hat of the male dancer. After approximately 15 seconds from the start of the dance, the computer answers by speech synthesizer; if the dance is a waltz, the synthesizer announces "This is [a] waltz." At the same time, MIDI instruments controlled by the computer play music to accompany the dance, and the systems of the musical score are shown on the CRT display one by one in order. Dance steps used in the present experiment have been limited to the six ballroom dances: the waltz, tango, slow fox-trot, quick step, Viennese waltz, and blues. The standard pattern of each dance step can be updated by a learning method.

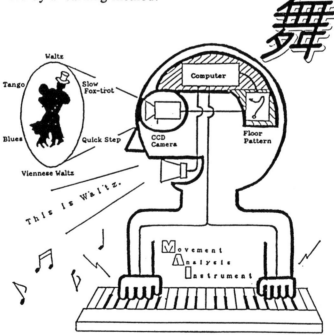

Schematic diagram of the computerized dance-step recognition and musical accompaniment system *Movement Analysis Instrument MAI*.

The continuum of the movements made in dancing is not governed by physical time but by the time passage expressed in the musical score. Indeed, almost all dance notations are expressed with the musical score as the time base. This system can display in real time the musical score and the corresponding movement vectors (velocity and acceleration) as the dance pattern-recognition output in real time. This output may be called "dynamic" orchesography or choreography.

a:

b:

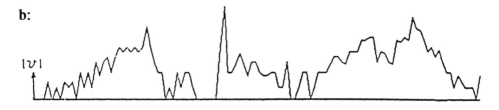

c:

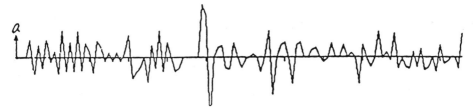

MAI's **dynamic choreography**, showing the velocity (b) and acceleration (c) vectors related to the score passage (a).

The present system not only is promising for harmonizing dance with computer music, but will also be applicable to the other performances in which movement and music are combined, such as the automatization of the musical accompaniment for animation, or for synchronized swimming. In this connection, we are trying to read Laban notation [for dance choreography] automatically, using our vision system. This attempt may be considered to be an inverse transformation experiment of the above dancing system.

REFERENCES

Calvert, T. W. "Toward a Language for Human Movement," *Computers and the Humanities*, 20/1 (1986), 35-43.

Hutchinson, A. *Dance Notation*. New York: Dance Horizons, 1984.

Namekawa, N., T. Furukawa, S. Ohteru, and S. Hashimoto. "Computerized Dance-step Recognition and Musical Accompaniment," *Convention Record of the Acoustical Society of Japan*, 1989 [in Japanese].

Rokeby, David. "Body Language," *ACM Siggraph Art Show, August 1-5, 1988, Atlanta*.

Sadamu Ohteru *is in the Department of Applied Physics, Waseda University, 3-4-1 Okubo, Shinjuku-ku, Tokyo 169, Japan; tel. +81-3-203-4141; fax 3-200-2567; e-mail: SOHTERU@ JPNWAS00.AC.JP.*

Hong Kong: Automatic Arrangement of Popular Song Melodies

A project on automatic arrangement of popular song melodies [mentioned in last year's issue of *CM*, p. 115] continues at Hong Kong Polytechnic. A deterministic algorithm for finding a rhythmic pattern to accompany a given popular song melody has been developed; the results have been found to be satisfactory. In order to further improve the results, heuristics are needed for the system. Local popular song arrangers are now being invited to help to identify these heuristics.

A simple deterministic auto-harmonization system has also been developed. This system accepts a popular song melody input from the keyboard and assigns chords to it. The melody is analyzed by an algorithmic approach and the appropriate chords are determined by a rule-based approach. A searching algorithm has been used so that an optimal solution can be determined in an efficient way. The chords so determined are sounded together with the melody as the output of the system. While the results of this system were found to be satisfactory by local popular-song arrangers, heuristics incorporated into the system were inadequate and the types of chords used were not sufficiently versatile. Work is now being carried out to improve performance in these areas.

These projects were originally commercially oriented, but the theories and concepts used originate in the computer science field. The auto-harmonization system had been implemented as a final year project of the Computer Science Department at the Hong Kong Polytechnic. It is anticipated that the whole automatic arrangement project, when completed, will be sufficient to produce a thesis in either the computer science field or the music field.

REFERENCES

Chin, Francis, and Stephen Wu. "An Efficient Algorithm for Rhythm Finding," *Computer Music Journal*, forthcoming.

Stephen Wu *can be reached at the Computer Science Department, University of Hong Kong, Hong Kong; tel. +852 715-7466; e-mail: swu@csd.hku.hk.*

Byrd's Book of Notational Records: Provisional Answers

These answers to the questions appearing on p. 24 are provisional ones submitted by Don Byrd. Readers are encouraged to submit their own answers. C4 = Middle C; A0 = the lowest note of the piano; C8 = the highest note of the piano.

1. *Longest movement in measures?* Schubert, Symphony No. 9, movement IV, has 1154 measures.

2. *Longest movement in time?* No conjectures; all answers may be subjective.

3. *Largest number of written notes?* This should be an easy number-crunching task for most programs, but at present we have no statistics.

4. *Most ledger lines above staff?* Nine (C8) in Don Martino's *Pianississimo*.

5. *Most ledger lines below staff?* Six (for B0 or A0) in such works as Brahms's Op. 79 and Prokofiev's Op. 11.

6. *Highest sounding pitch?* C#8 (in harmonics) in Schoenberg's Violin Concerto.

7. *Lowest sounding pitch?* F0 in Bartók's Rhapsody, Op. 1.

8. *Shortest notated duration?* 256th notes in Vivaldi's Concerto for *Flautino* RV 544 (F.IV/5).

9. *Longest notated duration including ties?* Equivalent to 35 whole notes in Beethoven's Symphony No. 9, movement II, basses. Bartók's *The Wooden Prince* opens with 120 measures of tied dotted halves of timpani roll.

10. *Most augmentation dots?* Quadruple dots on a half note are found in Bartók's *Music for Strings, Percussion, and Celesta*, movement III, and in Hindemith's *Mathis der Maler* Symphony, movement III, introduction.

11. *Most complex tuplet?* Three-level nested tuplets (3:4, 7:8, 3) are found in Stockhausen's *Klavierstücke I*.

12. *Most notes or chords in one beam set?* Liszt's *Transcendental Etude* No. 4 ("Mazeppa") contains 132 events broken across three systems. This set contains 15 secondary beam breaks and 28 segments.

13. *Most p's?* Six (**pppppp**) are found in the bassoon part of Tchaikovsky's Symphony No. 6, movement I, m. 160.

14. *Most f's?* Five (**fffff**) are found in Henze's Barcarolla for Large Orchestra, near the end in several parts, and in the last chord of the piano part (where it may overstated by one) in Ives's *Putnam's Camp* (from *Three Places in New England*).

15. *Most staves in a system?* 61 near the end of Carter's Concerto for Orchestra (1969).

16. *Greatest number of simultaneously notated parts?* 69 are present on the same page cited in the preceding answer.

17. *Most notes on a single stem?* Nine in *Putnam's Camp* [see #14].

18. *Most notes in a vertical simultaneity?* No entries at this time.

Music Notation Software

Edmund Correia, Jr.

Each spring CCARH sends out to several dozen developers of music notation software a packet of musical examples exhibiting passages which are problematic from a typographical point of view while being essential from a musicological perspective. The developers have a window of approximately three months' time in which to respond with their own settings of selected examples. The solicitation is accompanied by a form requesting specific information about the hardware and software environment in which the program is run. This information is used in compiling the short descriptions that appear at the end of this section.

Developers often report in detail on those aspects of their products that are especially competitive. Heavily advertised products that are listed but not shown here are missing because no contribution has been made. We also include mention of products that we learned of too late to include in our solicitation, especially if we believe they may be of value in the setting of difficult repertories. Some printing capabilities built into broad-spectrum MIDI programs are not oriented towards the needs of classical music, and these programs are only therefore represented if such a capability is demonstrated.

Some developers respond every year; others prefer to respond only when new features have been added to their programs. Most software for printing classical music comes from small firms with few employees. Inconveniently timed illnesses, manpower shortages, equipment failures, or relocations may prevent them from responding punctually.

Over the seven years in which we have made this solicitation, the quality and availability of programs to print music have been enormously increased, but some of the issues in which users take the most interest remain incompletely addressed. Readers of *CM* are therefore encouraged to consult earlier issues to get a more complete picture of these issues. Those consulting earlier issues will see that the examples of previous years have taken on a life of their own in advertising copy.

Since all developers are virtuosos at operating their own programs and since no information is provided here on the human interface of each program represented, the difficulty of duplicating the illustrations is a separate matter from assessing the quality of the output. Readers are urged to test programs personally before buying them.

Comments on the Illustrations

In our relentless search for ever greater typographical challenges, it was feared that perhaps this year's examples had gone beyond being vexing into the realm of the cruel and unusual. Apparently, we will have to look beyond the turn of the last century to exhaust the industry and resourcefulness of our contributors. Once again they have responded abundantly and with generally excellent quality to our solicitation. Some even expressed their gratitude for the opportunity to put their systems to such a severe test, noting that a few well-hidden bugs were thus brought to light.

The sources of the excerpts are works composed within a 20-year period, 1890-1910. They are as follows: (1) Brahms's *Clarinet Quintet*, (2) *Das Lied von der Erde* of Mahler (vocal score), and (3) Ravel's *Gaspard de la nuit*, famous for stretching the limits of pianistic virtuosity.

The chief difficulty encountered in the Brahms quintet proved to be the extreme measure length coupled with very short note values. The space restrictions imposed by our page size and margins undoubtedly discouraged many from attempting a setting.

The freedom to make reasonable cuts was exercised to better advantage in the Mahler and Ravel excerpts. The Mahler, somewhat similar to last year's Wagner example, has several tricky rhythmic alignments, particularly the 4:5:6 ratio in the bar immediately preceding rehearsal number 34. Beams that cross bar lines and staves, highly eccentric slurs, and a truly spectacular collision (Bar 10) did not deter a large proportion of our contributors from submitting a Ravel setting. Let it simply be stated that no oath was required swearing that all slurs were purely computer-generated.

This year we invited a traditional typesetter, Melvin Wildberger, to submit a few samples of his work. We thought it would be interesting to contrast his approach to that of today's leading programmers. He did not disappoint us. See p. 171 for Mr. Wildberger's own comments on his work.

In the free choice category, the markup needs required to express historical and analytical points add significantly to the complexity of the examples submitted by Don Giller and John William Schaffer as third-party contributions. Giller also calls attention to the coincidental capabilities of a popular publishing program to produce chant notation. An excerpt from George Crumb's *Makrokosmos* presents the need for acrobatic feats, which are easily handled by *Amadeus*.

List of Illustrations

The numbered illustrations are arranged alphabetically (1) by the surname of the composer and (2) by the surname of the contributor. Illustrations are unretouched. Printer designations identify the specific configuration used to produce the example. Most programs can interface with several printers and some run on multiple platforms, but the results are not necessarily uniform. The originating hardware is indicated in this listing.

Brahms: *Clarinet Quintet*, **Op. 115 (1891): Adagio.** Excerpt taken from the *Sämtliche Werke* (Leipzig: Breitkopf und Härtel, 1927), VII.

1. Excerpt distributed
2. IBM PC clone — *DARMS Interpreter*
3. IBM PC — *The Note Processor*
4. Macintosh II — *HB Music Engraver/Illustrator*
5. Macintosh — *Lime*
6. Archimedes workstation — *Philip's Music Scribe*
7. Atari ST — *Notator*
8. Erato workstation — *Erato Music Manuscriptor*
9. IBM PC — *SCORE*

Mahler: *Das Lied von der Erde*, **"Der Abschied."** Taken from the vocal score by Erwin Stein (London: Universal Edition, 1911).

10. Excerpt distributed
11. Macintosh — *Nightingale*
12. IBM PC clone — *DARMS Interpreter*
13. IBM PC — *The Note Processor*
14. Archimedes workstation — *Philip's Music Scribe*
15. IBM PC — *L.M.P. Prima*
16. Atari ST — *Notator*
17. NEC PC-9801 — *Dai Nippon Music Processor*
18. IBM PC — *MusicEase*
19. Synclavier — *Synclavier Music Engraving System*
20. Traditional typesetting — *Musicwriter*
21. Sun workstation (Sun-3 or SPARC) — *MusE*

Ravel: *Gaspard de la nuit: 3 Poèmes pour piano d'après Aloysius Bertrand,* "Scarbo"
(Paris: Editions Durand & Cie, 1909).

22. Excerpt distributed	
23. Macintosh II	*HB Music Engraver/Illustrator*
24. IBM PC	*L.M.P Prima*
25. Atari Mega ST4 or TT	*Amadeus*
26. NEC PC-9801	*Dai Nippon Music Processor*
27. Erato workstation	*Erato Music Manuscriptor*
28. IBM PC	*SCORE*
29. Synclavier	*Synclavier Music Engraving System*
30. Traditional typesetting	*Musicwriter*
31. Sun workstation (Sun-3 or SPARC)	*MusE*

Free choices:

32. Medieval music with interpretive symbols [Macintosh II]	*HB Music Engraver*
33. Plainchant [Macintosh II]	*Adobe Illustrator*
34. George Crumb: "Leo" [Atari Mega ST4 or TT]	*Amadeus*
35. Chopin Mazurka—analytical reduction [Macintosh]	*NoteWriter II*
36. Wolpe Quartet—Set-theoretic readings [Macintosh]	*NoteWriter II*

The listing of *Current and Recent Contributors* appears on pp. 159-172.

Illustration 1
Brahms: *Clarinet Quintet*, Op. 115
Excerpt sent to software developers

Illustration 2

Contributor: John Dunn

Product: *DARMS Interpreter (Comus)*

Running on: IBM PC compatibles (UNIX System V)

Output from: HP LaserJet clone (300 dpi)

Size as shown: 92% of original

Illustration 3

Contributor: Stephen Dydo   **Output from:** Imagesetter
Product: *The Note Processor*   **Size as shown:** 100% of original
Running on: IBM PC compatibles   **Engraver:** Susan Altabet

Illustration 4

Contributor: Don Giller   **Output from:** Linotronic L-300
Product: *HB Music Engraver/Adobe Illustrator*   **Size as shown:** 100% of original
Running on: Apple Macintosh II

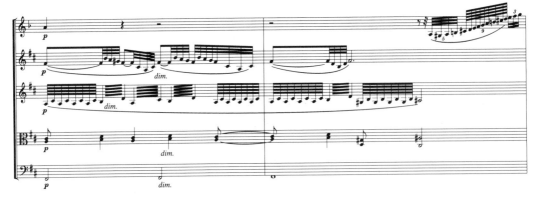

Illustration 5

Contributor: Lippold Haken
Product: *Lime*
Running on: Apple Macintosh

Output from: Apple Laserwriter
Size as shown: 75% of original

Illustration 6

Contributor: Philip Hazel
Product: *Philip's Music Scribe*
Running on: Acorn Archimedes workstation

Output from: Apple Laserwriter
Size as shown: 80% of original

Illustration 7

Contributor: Robert Hunt

Product: *Notator SL*

Running on: Atari ST series

Output from: Atari Laserprinter

Size as shown: 80% of original

Illustration 8

Contributor: Jeffrey L. Price
Product: *Erato Music Manuscriptor*
Running on: Erato workstation

Output from: HP LaserJet II
Size as shown: 100% of original

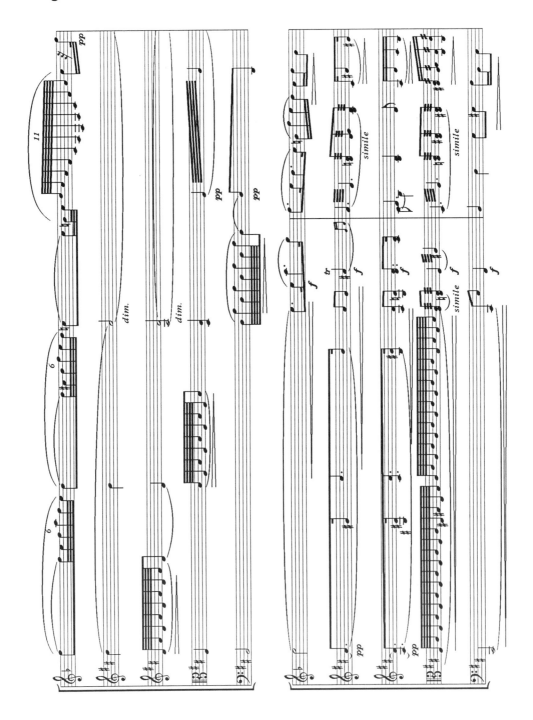

Illustration 9

Contributor: Leland Smith
Product: *SCORE*
Running on: IBM PC compatibles

Output from: Varityper-600
Size as shown: 56% of original

Illustration 10
Mahler: "Der Abschied" *Das Lied von der Erde*
Excerpt sent to software developers

Illustration 11

Contributor: Donald Byrd
Product: *Nightingale*
Running on: Apple Macintosh

Output from: Linotronic L-300
Size as shown: 100% of original
Engravers: Tim Crawford, John Gibson

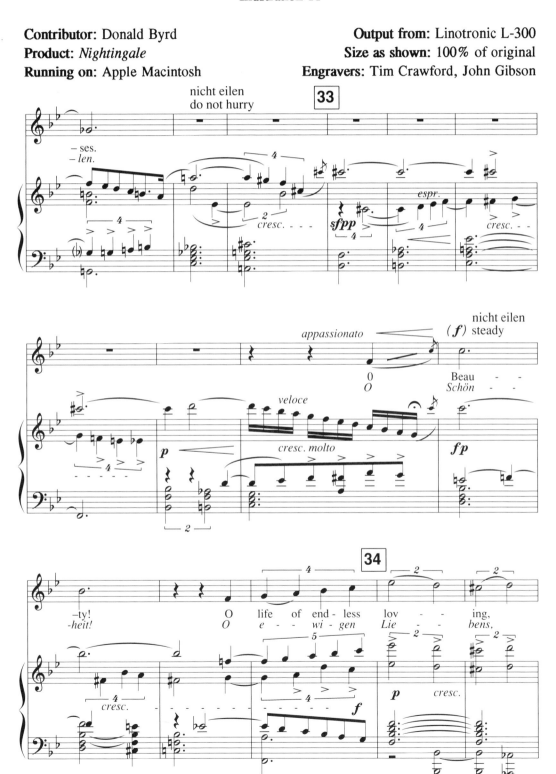

Illustration 12

Contributor: John Dunn   **Output from:** HP LaserJet clone (300 dpi)
Product: *DARMS Interpreter (Comus)*   **Size as shown:** 92% of original
Running on: IBM PC compatibles (UNIX System V)

Illustration 13

Contributor: Stephen Dydo   **Output from:** Imagesetter
Product: *The Note Processor*   **Size as shown:** 100% of original
Running on: IBM PC compatibles   **Engraver:** Susan Altabet

Illustration 14

Contributor: Philip Hazel

Product: *Philip's Music Scribe*

Running on: Acorn Archimedes workstation

Output from: Apple Laserwriter

Size as shown: 100% of original

Illustration 15

Contributor: Gary Hullquist
Product: *L.M.P. Prima*
Running on: IBM PC compatibles

Output from: HP LaserJet
Size as shown: 82.5% of original

Illustration 16

Contributor: Robert Hunt   **Output from:** Atari Laserprinter
Product: *Notator SL*   **Size as shown:** 70% of original
Running on: Atari ST series

Illustration 17

Contributor: Kentaro Oka
Product: *Dai Nippon Music Processor*
Running on: NEC PC-9801

Output from: Digiset typesetter
Size as shown: 79% of original

Illustration 18

Contributor: Gary M. Rader   **Output from:** HP LaserJet III
Product: *MusicEase*   **Size as shown:** 60% of original
Running on: IBM PC compatibles

Illustration 19

Contributor: Alan D. Talbot   **Output from:** Agfa Compugraphic 9400
Product: *Synclavier Music Engraving System*   **Size as shown:** 100% of original
Running on: *Synclavier Music Engraving System*   **Engraver:** Gregg Sewell

Illustration 20

Contributor: Melvin Wildberger   **Output from:** *Musicwriter*

Size as shown: 100% of original

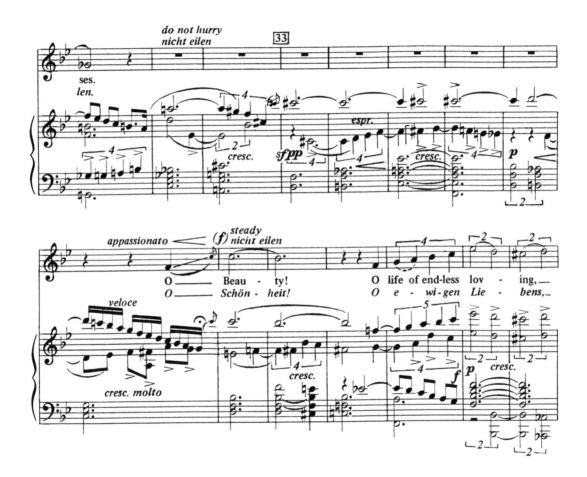

Music typesetting by Mel Wildberger using a *Musicwriter* music typewriter, IBM *Standalone* composer, pen, ink, and templates.

Illustration 21

Contributor: Rolf Wulfsberg
Product: *MusE*
Running on: Sun-3 or SPARC station

Output from: Linotype L-300
Size as shown: 100% of original

Illustration 22
Ravel: "Scarbo" from *Gaspard de la nuit*
Excerpt sent to software developers

The last system may be omitted if necessary.

Illustration 23

Contributor: Don Giller

Product: *HB Music Engraver/Adobe Illustrator*

Running on: Apple Macintosh II

Output from: Linotronic L-300

Size as shown: 100% of original

Illustration 24

Contributor: Gary Hullquist
Product: *L.M.P. Prima*
Running on: IBM PC compatibles

Output from: HP LaserJet
Size as shown: 82.5% of original

Illustration 25

Contributor: Kurt Maas

Product: *Amadeus*

Running on: Atari Mega ST4 or TT

Output from: ECRM typesetter

Size as shown: 90% of original

Illustration 26

Contributor: Kentaro Oka
Product: *Dai Nippon Music Processor*
Running on: NEC PC-9801

Output from: Digiset typesetter
Size as shown: 79% of original

Illustration 27

Contributor: Jeffrey L. Price
Product: *Erato Music Manuscriptor*
Running on: Erato workstation

Output from: HP LaserJet II
Size as shown: 100% of original

Illustration 28

Contributor: Leland Smith
Product: *SCORE*
Running on: IBM PC compatibles

Output from: Varityper-600
Size as shown: 56% of original

Illustration 29

Contributor: Alan D. Talbot   **Output from:** Agfa Compugraphic 9400
Product: *Synclavier Music Engraving System*   **Size as shown:** 100% of original
Running on: *Synclavier Music Engraving System*   **Engraver:** Gregg Sewell

Illustration 30

Contributor: Melvin Wildberger

Output from: *Musicwriter*
Size as shown: 100% of original

Music typesetting by Mel Wildberger using a *Musicwriter* music typewriter, IBM *Standalone* composer, pen, ink, and templates.

Illustration 31

Contributor: Rolf Wulfsberg
Product: *MusE*
Running on: Sun-3 or SPARC station

Output from: Linotype L-300
Size as shown: 100% of original

Illustrations 32a and b
Medieval polyphonic music

Contributor: Don Giller   **Output from:** Linotronic L-300
Product: *HB Music Engraver/Adobe Illustrator*   **Size as shown:** 100% of original
Running on: Apple Macintosh II

a:

b:

Illustration 33
Medieval monophonic music

Contributor: Don Giller
Product: *Adobe Illustrator*
Running on: Apple Macintosh II

Output from: Linotronic L-300
Size as shown: 100% of original

Illustrations 32a and b and 33 appeared in *Studies in Medieval Music: Festschrift for Ernest H. Sanders, Current Musicology*, 45-7 (1990). 32a shows a discant reduction of "A Christo honoratus" in Sarah Fuller's article on modal tenors in Machaut motets (p. 235). 32b shows the clausula "Et Iherusalem" from the thirteenth-century *Magnus Liber Organi* (with a variant rhythmic interpretation above) in Norman E. Brown's study (p. 295) of notation in *fractio modi* in interrelated clausulae and motets. 33 shows variant readings in thirteenth- and fourteenth-century graduals of the Christmas chant "Puer natus" in Alexander Blachly's study (p. 107) of "Germanic" plainchant.

Illustration 34

George Crumb: *Makrokosmos 1* (1974)

Contributor: Kurt Maas   **Output from:** ECRM typesetter

Product: *Amadeus*   **Size as shown:** 115% of original

Running on: Atari Mega ST4 or TT

8. The Magic Circle of Infinity (Moto Perpetuo).   Symbol: Leo

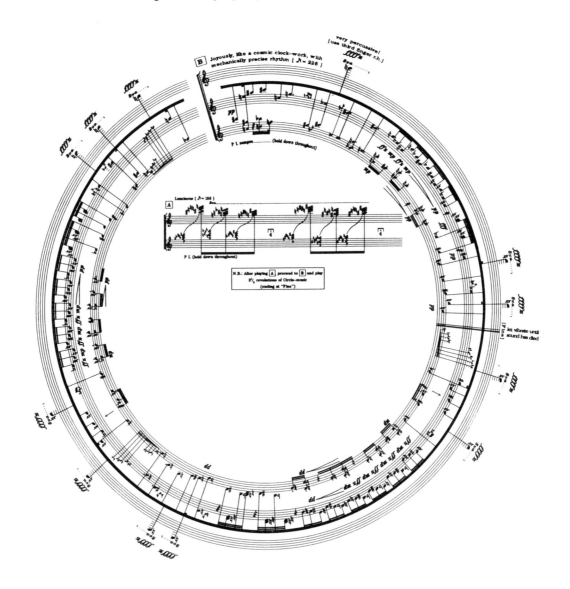

Illustration 35
Chopin: Mazurka No. 43—Analytical examples

Contributor: John William Schaffer
Product: *NoteWriter II*
Running on: Apple Macintosh

Output from: unspecified
Size as shown: 75% of original

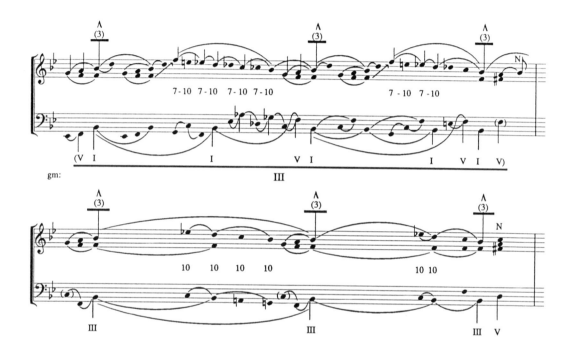

Illustration 36
Wolpe: String Quartet (1969)—Analytical examples

Contributor: John William Schaffer   **Output from:** unspecified

Product: *NoteWriter II*   **Size as shown:** 85% of original

Running on: Apple Macintosh

Example 7.3: Hasty's Segmentation of Wolpe, *String Quartet* (1969), m.1

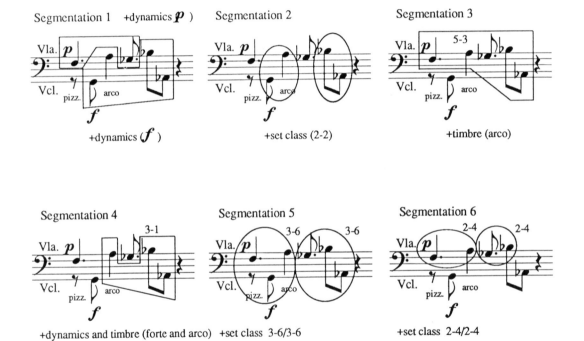

Current and Recent Contributors

This listing concentrates on systems that have been represented by illustrations over the past three years and incorporates definitions of terms needed to understand the accounts given. Additional systems that are now dormant were cited in earlier issues. Several developers (and their products) who have not contributed in recent years can be found in the 1990 volume of *CM*, pp. 62-73. Music printing programs advertised in popular music magazines are listed here only if they have a demonstrated capability for handling classical music of moderate complexity.

A-R Music Engraver. See *MusE*.

Alpha/TIMES. Rehetobelstr. 89, CH-9016 St. Gallen, Switzerland; tel. +41 71-35-1402. An integrated input and analysis system by Christoph Schnell for the Apple Macintosh line. *TIMES* stands for *Totally Integrated Musicological Environment System.* An unusual input method (voice-recognition device with light pen) permits accurate reproduction of non-common notation, including neumes. The system incorporates graphics editors, a font editor, and a communication system [see p. 10]. Illustrated in 1988 and previous years.

Amadeus [pp. 147, 156]. Amadeus Music Software GmbH, Rohrauerstr. 50, Postfach 710267, W-8000 München 71, Germany; tel. +49 89-7854750. This product, originally developed by Kurt Maas, is commercially available for the Atari Mega ST4 or TT. Both alphanumeric and MIDI input are supported, the latter facilitating acoustical playback. Most data are stored as ASCII files. Screen editing is provided. Output (for dot matrix and laser printers, plotters, and phototypesetters) is scalable to a resolution of 1000 dots per inch.

Berlioz. Logiciel "Berlioz", Place des Lavoirs, F-30350 Lédignan, France; tel. +33 66-83-46-53. This is a series of three programs written in *C* by Dominique Montel and Frédéric Magiera. They run on the Macintosh. The first program is for input, the second for layout, and the third for graphic editing. Input is created graphically. Extensive provisions for layout and graphic editing are provided. PostScript files for output to laser printers and phototypesetters are generated. *Berlioz*, which is in use at the printing establishment s.a.r.l. Dominique Montel, is also available for licensing. Illustrated in 1990.

Calliope. *Calliope* is a UNIX-based printing program developed by William Clocksin at the University of Cambridge (Computing Laboratory, New Museums Site, Pembroke St.,

Cambridge, CB2 3QG, UK). Although we learned about it too late to include examples in this year's issue, we are reliably informed that *Calliope* has extensive capabilities for printing early repertories. It has recently been used to produce a score of Stefano Landi's opera *Sant'Alessio* of 1634. Currently running under *X Windows* on Sun workstations, *Calliope* will be adapted to other UNIX environments in the coming year.

CCARH [p. 31]. CCARH, 525 Middlefield Rd., Ste. 120, Menlo Park, CA 94025; tel. (415) 322-7050; email: XB.L36@Stanford.Bitnet. The Center's music representation system supports the development of electronic transcriptions and editions of a large quantity of musical repertory, chiefly from the sixteenth through the eighteenth centuries. Input of pitch and duration information is from an electronic keyboard; alphanumeric code is used to provide non-acoustical information. A provisional description is available from CCARH. A corollary music printing system, developed by Walter B. Hewlett, has been used to produce performing scores of major works by Handel [*cf.* p. 32] and Telemann. These capabilities are currently being implemented on a UNIX workstation. CCARH's input code was shown in the *1987 Directory*, p. 20.

Comus [pp. 124, 134]. Comus Music Printing and Publishing, Armthorpe, Tixall, Stafford ST18 0XP, England; tel. +44 0785-662520. The proprietary music printing program developed by John Dunn for this firm uses *DARMS* encoding of data with some newly devised extensions. The current version produces device-independent output in UNIX plot(5) format, which can be directed to screens, plotters, and laser printers.

The Copyist III. Dr. T's Music Software, 220 Boylston St., Suite 260, Chestnut Hill, MA 02167; tel. (617) 244-6954. Three versions of this commercial program for Atari, Amiga, and IBM PC compatibles are offered by Dr. T's. "III" is the most comprehensive version and the one best suited to academic applications. MIDI input and output are supported. Files, which are edited graphically on the screen, can be converted to *Tagged Image File Format* (*TIFF*), a compressed representation of graphics information, and *Encapsulated PostScript* (*EPS*). Output to PostScript and Ultrascript printers as well as the Hewlett Packard LaserJet Plus and plotters is supported. *The Copyist* interfaces with a number of popular sequencer and publishing programs. The developer is Crispin Sion. Illustrated in 1990 and preceding years.

Cubase. Steinberg Jones, 17700 Raymer St., Ste. 1001, Northridge, CA 91325; tel. (818) 993-4091. This program for the Atari ST is primarily a sequencer, with a focus on MIDI data input and real-time editing, but it also features modest scoring capabilities. Dynamics, slurs, text, and other symbols may be added to the transcribed MIDI data with a mouse. Most 9- and 24-pin printers are supported as well as the Atari Laserprinter, HP

LaserJet and HP DeskJet. A 1991 free-choice submission by Ron Sorter could not be used because copyright status could not be ascertained. Illustrated in 1989.

Dai Nippon Music Processor [p. 148]. Dai Nippon Printing Co., Ltd., CTS Division, 1-1 Ichigaya-kagacho 1-chome, Shinjuku-ku, Tokyo 162-01, Japan; fax +81 03-3266-4199. This dedicated hardware system for the production of musical scores was announced four years ago and illustrations were provided in 1988 and 1990. Input is alphanumeric. Screen editing is supported. Output files can be sent to MIDI instruments, to PostScript printers, to a Digiset typesetter, or to the *Standard Music Expression* (*SMX*) file format used in music research at Waseda University. Kentaro Oka, the author of a recent article [*cf.* p. 20] on the use of Standard Generalized Markup Language for music documents, is the current manager.

Darbellay Music Processor. See **WOLFGANG**.

DARMS is an encoding system that originated in the 1960's. Various dialects have been used in several printing programs including those of A-R Editions, *The Note Processor*, *Comus*, and systems developed at the State University of New York at Binghamton by Harry Lincoln and at the University of Nottingham, England, by John Morehen. A sample of the code was shown in the *1987 Directory*, p. 12.

DXF. See *Graphics file formats*.

DynaDuet. DynaWare, 950 Tower Lane #1150, Foster City, CA 94404; tel. (415) 349-5700. *DynaDuet*, a music printing program by Chris Geen for the IBM PC, accepts MIDI or alphanumeric input. The program's capabilities for classical music printing are under development. Output for 24-pin dot matrix printers is provided.

EASY KEY. John Clifton, 175 W. 87th St., Ste. 27E, New York, NY 10024; tel. (212) 724-1578. *Easy Key* simplifies the use of Jim Miller's *Personal Composer* input and printing program.

EPS. See *Graphics file formats*.

ERATO Music Manuscriptor. See under *Music Manuscriptor*.

ESCORT. Passport Designs, 625 Miramontes Street, Half Moon Bay, CA 94019; tel. (415) 726-0280. *Escort* facilitates input from a MIDI device to the *SCORE* printing program published by Passport.

ESTAFF. A notation program for single-voiced melodies. It automatically translates any file encoded in *ESAC* [*cf.* pp. 30-2] into conventional staff notation, and is compatible with the Essen *MAPPET* files (now numbering some 13,000 documented melodies). *ESTAFF* can also be used to write notes onto a blank staff, custom design musical graphics, and even convert Western notation into Chinese Jianpu notation with automatic text underlay. Other features include text, print, graphics, and playback options. Available free by license to interested researchers. For more information please contact Helmut Schaffrath at the Universität Essen, FB 4 - Musik - Postfach, W-4300 Essen 1, Germany; email: *JMP100@DE0HRZ1A.BITNET.*

EUTERPE [p. 61]. 99 rue Frédéric Mistral, F-03100 Montluçon, France; tel. +33 70-036903. *Euterpe* is a printing system under development by Michel Wallet. It forms part of an integrated system for encoding, printing, and analysis on the Macintosh. Special attention has been devoted to lute music and late Byzantine music. Transcription and conversion capabilities for German lute tablature to staff notation, based on programs by Bernard Stepien, were shown in 1988. The printing of Byzantine notation with text underlay in Cyrillic characters was shown in 1990. See related commentary on pp. 60-4.

FASTCODE. An encoding language of the 1970's developed at Princeton University for white mensural notation. An example of plotter output from 1981, first shown in 1985, was repeated in 1990.

Finale. Coda Music Software, Wenger Music Learning Systems, 1401 E. 79th St., Bloomington, MN 55420-1126; tel. (612) 854-1288. *Finale* has a broad range of capabilities related to music transcription and printing. MIDI files can be imported and exported. It provides immediate screen transcription of two-handed music. Four-part works played in two-stave arrangements may be "exploded" into four parts. Conversely, multi-voice music can be "imploded" to a piano reduction. Versions for the Macintosh and PC compatibles are currently available; a version for the NeXT is under development. Data may also be entered alphanumerically. Finale's *Enigma Transportable Files* (*ETF*) are text files used to facilitate printing [Robert Gjerdingen will write about *Enigma* files in a forthcoming issue of *Computers in Music Research*]. *MusicProse* is a subset of *Finale* features made available at reduced cost and generally suited more to popular than to classical music.

Coda offers several music fonts—*Petrucci* for conventional notation, *Rameau* for subscripted chord names and basso continuo figures, *Seville* for guitar tablature, and *Newport* for jazz and percussion notation. *Finale* also provides support for mensural notation. PostScript printers are supported. *Finale* is being used to prepare the complete works of Andrea Gabrieli and G. B. Pergolesi.

Phil Ferrand developed the original program. Tim Herzog contributed illustrations in 1989 but has now left the firm, which has since failed to respond to enquiries.

Giller, Don [pp. 126, 154-5]. 300 W. 106th St. #22, New York, NY 10025; tel. (212) 663-0515. Don Giller has been working as a freelance music book editor and music and math desktop publisher since 1985. The examples contributed to the present volume were mainly created using *HB Music Engraver* on a Macintosh II. Giller prefers Adobe's *Sonata* font to HB's proprietary *Interlude* and exports each music file directly into Adobe's *Illustrator*, a PostScript graphics program, in which any individual component may be modified or corrected, and where components best produced by a graphics program can be added. The neumes in Illustration 33 were created directly in *Illustrator*.

Graphic Notes. See *Music Publisher*.

Graphics file formats. The scaling of notation, the integration of musical examples in text files, and the interchange of music printing files between programs are three capabilities that depend, in many computer environments, on the ability to export notation files via a recognized graphics file format to external programs. Many such formats are in use. Those most commonly cited by our contributors are *DXF*, which supports *AutoCAD*; *Encapsulated PostScript* (*EPS*), which creates files for a PostScript printer; *HPGL*, which creates a Hewlett-Packard Graphics Language plotter file; *PC Paintbrush* format (*PCX*); and *Tagged Image File Format* (*TIFF*).

HB Music Engraver. Formerly offered by HB Imaging, Inc., of Orem, UT. Last known address: 1520 S. 280 East, Orem UT 84058; no telephone support now available. This printing program runs on the Apple Macintosh and produces output for PostScript printers. Input is alphanumeric and utilizes redefinition of the QWERTY keyboard. No direct contribution has been received in recent years. For examples of what the program can do, see pp. 126 and 154.

HPGL. See *Graphics file formats*.

Humdrum *scor. See p. 67.

HyperScribe. Coda Music Software, Wenger Music Learning Systems, 1401 E. 79th St., Bloomington, MN 55420-1126; tel. (612) 854-1288. This product transcribes MIDI input to a Macintosh screen. It complements other products from Coda, such as *Finale*.

Interactive Music System (IMS). CERL Music Group, University of Illinois, 103 S. Mathews #252, Urbana, IL 61801-2977; tel. (217) 333-0766. This multi-faceted system has been under development at the University of Illinois since the early 1970's. It originated on the PLATO system; extensions for the Macintosh and other microcomputers have been made in recent years. Music can be input from an alphanumeric code or from a synthesizer. Its printing capability was last shown in 1987, when its input and intermediate codes were given on pp. 18-9. A commercial version, *Lime* [see below], is now available for the Macintosh.

la mà de guido [Guido's Hand]. Apartat 23, E-08200, Sabadell (Barcelona), Spain; tel. +34 3-716-1350. This music printing software for IBM PC XT and AT computers uses an alphanumeric input system based on a redefined QWERTY keyboard (shown in the *1988 Directory*, p. 48). It is now being marketed as an input system for *SCORE*. MIDI playback and analysis are supported. Graphic output is by *HPGL* plotter or for PostScript printers of resolutions up to 2700 dpi. The developer is Llorenç Balsach.

Lime [p. 127]. CERL Sound Group, University of Illinois, 103 S. Mathews #252, Urbana, IL 61801-2977; fax (217) 244-0793. This newly released Macintosh version of the *Interactive Music System* (see above) music printing program was developed at the University of Illinois and at Queen's University (Kingston, Ontario) by Lippold Haken and Dorothea Blostein. A beta-test version has been used to create the score and parts for a 1989 production of Vivaldi's *Orlando furioso* and to prepare a catalogue of music holdings of the Accademia Filarmonica in Bologna. For information on obtaining a free demonstration copy of *Lime* by ftp over Internet, send electronic mail to *L-Haken@uiuc.edu*. A description of *Lime*'s music representation is also available to the public.

L.M.P. Prima [pp. 137, 146]. TEACH Services, 182 Donivan Rd., Brushton, NY 12916; tel. (518) 358-2125. This version of *L.M.P.* (*Laser Music Processor*) for IBM PC and compatibles is still under development. It is intended for commercial distribution. Note entry is by computer keyboard, mouse, standard MIDI file transcription or MIDI device. MIDI-device entry may be direct to screen (step time) or to file in real time. Printing in both portrait and landscape modes is available for laser users. More than 400 symbols are available. Dot-matrix printers can produce draft and high-resolution (240 dpi) output. A driver for the Hewlett Packard DeskJet is available as well as print-to-file and *PC Paintbrush* (*PCX*) image-file formats.

MTeX is a set of fonts for music typesetting with the TeX document description language on mainframe computers. They were developed by Angelika Schofer and Andrea

Steinbach at the Rheinische Friedrich-Wilhelms-Universität in Bonn. The set is available for DM 25 at Wegler Strasse 6, D-5300 Bonn, Germany.

MusE [(formerly *A-R Music Engraver*; pp. 143, 153]. A-R Editions, Inc., 801 Deming Way, Madison, WI 53717; tel. (608) 836-9000. A commercial version of the music typesetting system used by this publisher for its own editions and musical examples for academic journals has been developed for professional music publishing and is now available by license. Tom Hall is the principal developer. This version of the program, for the UNIX operating system, uses the *NeWS* and *OpenWindows* interfaces on the Sun SPARC workstation with a high resolution monitor (1600 x 1280). A version for the Sun-3 is also available. Music input is done alphanumerically with a modified version of *DARMS*; files may be created on networked PC-AT compatibles. Music can be edited on the screen. Scanned images from Macintosh PostScript programs can be imported.

A music notation library developed by A-R and multiple text fonts created by Mergenthaler are cross-licensed and available for use with the program. PostScript printers and typesetters are supported. The output shown is 1270 dpi from a Linotron L-300.

Music Manuscriptor [pp. 130, 149]. Erato Software Corp., PO Box 6278, Salt Lake City, UT 84152-6278; tel. (801) 328-0500. This program operates as part of an integrated workstation for composition and orchestration. Setup requires an IBM PC compatible microcomputer, a digitizer tablet, and special graphics boards supporting a resolution of 800 x 1000 pixels. Pitches are entered as MIDI data; rhythmic assignment is automatic. Pattern storage (1000 slots) is provided for composition. Text underlay is available. Lines and pages can be justified automatically. A Breitkopf and Härtel font is available.

This product is compatible with two desktop publishing programs, *Ventura Publisher* and *Aldus Pagemaker*. Two laser printers, the Canon LBP8-11 and the Hewlett Packard LaserJet II, are supported. Erato takes pride in the efficiency of its database design. The sizes of the uncompressed files for the examples were as follows: Brahms—4.9 kilobytes, Mahler [not shown]—5.1 kilobytes, and Ravel—4.9 kilobytes.

Music Publisher. Repertoire Pty. Ltd., 49A Stephens Terrace, St. Peters, South Australia 5069, Australia; tel. +61 08-363-2600. The US distributor is InterSoft, 200 7th Ave., Suite 225, Santa Cruz, CA 95062; tel. (408) 476-1753. This program, developed by Trevor Richards for the Apple Macintosh, requires the use of a separate "presto pad" for input. It provides output for PostScript printers and typesetters. Examples were shown in 1988. No contribution has been provided since.

MusicEase [p. 140]. Grandmaster, Inc., PO Box 2567, Spokane, WA 99220-2567; tel. (509) 747-6773. This commercial product for IBM PC compatibles is primarily intended for on-screen assembly and editing of musical data, but it can also accept MIDI data in real time or step time. MIDI files may be imported and exported.

MusicPrinter Plus. Temporal Acuity Products, Inc., 300 - 120th Avenue N.E., Bldg. 1, Bellevue, WA 98005; tel. (800) 426-2673. TAP is a noted manufacturer of interactive systems for rhythmic drill and other music teaching products. Its music printing program, originally designed by Jack Jarrett, is for MS DOS machines. Version 4.0, which is MIDI compatible, permits double-staff input. The playback choices include real time and step time, which can be forward or backward; much subtlety of articulation is supported. Dot matrix, laser, and ink jet printers are supported. Wide-carriage output on the BJ-130 provides 360 dpi resolution. A submission was last received in 1989.

MusicProse. See *Finale*.

Musicwriter II. See *The Portable Musicwriter*.

MusiKrafters. MusiKrafters, PO Box 14124, Louisville, KY 40214; tel. (502) 361-4597. This software company offers special-purpose products by Robert Fruehwald for musical excerpts and unusual notations for the Apple Macintosh. Input is alphanumeric and may be edited on the screen. PostScript files are produced. Its shape-note and tablature capabilities were shown in 1988 and a *HyperText* program for musical information management was shown in 1989.

MusScribe. See *NoteWriter*.

MUSTRAN. This alphanumeric code was developed at Indiana University by Jerome Wenker in the 1960's. Music printing capabilities were extended by Don Byrd; music encoded in MUSTRAN has been used for analytical programs by Dorothy Gross, Gary Wittlich, and others.

Nightingale [p. 133]. Advanced Music Notation Systems, PO Box 60356, Florence, MA 01060; tel. (413) 586-3958. Don Byrd's program for music notation runs on the Apple Macintosh Plus. *Nightingale* uses MIDI input. Output may be edited graphically and further revised in popular desktop publishing programs. This year's contribution was produced by two beta-testers—Tim Crawford [*cf.* pp. 57-9] and John Gibson. Gibson is an independent engraver who uses *Nightingale* in contract work. He may be reached at 44 Vandevanter Ave. #3, Princeton, NJ 08540; tel. (609) 921-8905; e-mail:

gibson@silvertone.edu. During 1990-91, Byrd was in residence at the Center for Research on Concepts and Cognition, headed by Douglas Hofstadter, at Indiana University.

Notator [pp. 129, 138]. C-Lab Software GmbH, Postfach 700303, D-2000 Hamburg 70, Germany; tel. +49 040-694400-0. Technical support in the US is available from Robert Hunt; tel. (415) 738-1633. The design intent behind this software package for the Atari ST series was to combine advanced sequencing and notational capabilities in one product. As such, it stresses flexibility of input (primarily MIDI), editing control, efficient performance-to-printed-page interface, and overall ease of use. For those chiefly interested in notation, a junior version called *Alpha* is available, with the main difference being in the sequencer.

The Note Processor [pp. 125, 135]. Thoughtprocessors, 584 Bergen Street, Brooklyn, NY 11238; tel. (718) 857-2860. Stephen Dydo's program for IBM PC compatibles accepts both alphanumeric and MIDI input; data can be edited either through code revisions or on screen with a mouse. The input code is a dialect of *DARMS*; an example of *NP*'s representation scheme was shown in the *1987 Directory*, p. 13. Numerous dot matrix printers as well as the Hewlett Packard DeskJet and LaserJet printers are supported. MIDI output and file interchange with sequencer programs are supported. The *Engraver's Font Set* enables users to create their own symbols.

NoteWriter II [pp. 157-8]. Passport Designs, 625 Miramontes, Half Moon Bay, CA 94019; tel. (415) 726-0280. This commercial product for the Apple Macintosh is the heir of *MusScribe* (shown in 1988) and has been developed by Keith Hamel of Richmond, BC, Canada. *NoteWriter,* which is PostScript compatible, is used to typeset musical examples in several scholarly and popular music journals. *QuickScrawl* mode permits users to draw freehand. The system is described in "A General-Purpose Object-Oriented System for Musical Graphics," *Proceedings of the International Computer Music Conference 1989* (San Francisco: CMA, 1989), pp. 260-3. The analytical examples shown here were submitted by a user, John William Schaffer [*cf.* pp. 71-2].

Oberon Music Editor. Oberon Systems, PO Box 4179, Boulder, CO 80306-4179; tel. (303) 459-3411. This program for IBM PC compatibles is available as a stand-alone product or on a license basis. Entry is alphanumeric and supports printing only. A custom font, *Callisto*, and a multi-size font set called *Publisher Series* are available. A shape-note version of the editor is also available. Output devices supported include the Hewlett Packard LaserJet and DeskJet series as well as various 9- and 24-pin dot matrix printers. Musical examples can be integrated with *WordPerfect* files and output to

PostScript printers. Compatibility with *Ventura Publisher* is currently being implemented.

PCX. See *Graphics file formats*.

Personal Composer. Jim Miller, 3213 W. Wheeler St., Ste. 140, Seattle, WA 98199; tel. (206) 546-4800. Technical support is available by telephone at (206) 236-0105. This program by Jim Miller for the IBM PC line accepts MIDI and alphanumeric input and outputs PostScript files. While no contribution of music engraving has been received since 1987, evolving capabilities are regularly reported to CCARH. See also *Easy Key*.

Philip's Music Scribe (PMS) [pp. 128, 136]. 33 Metcalfe Road, Cambridge CB4 2DB, England; tel. +44 223-65518. This program by Philip Hazel for the Acorn Archimedes [UNIX] workstation uses alphanumeric input and produces PostScript files for output. Acorn products are currently available in the UK and Europe. *PMS*, which is now commercially available, has extensive capabilities for accommodating the needs of parts and scores derived from a common input file. Staves can be overlaid, permitting four-part choral music to be shown on two staves, for example. Up to four verses of text underlay can be accommodated. Slur control is extensive. Basso continuo figuration is supported. Time signatures can be switched off. All characters found in the *PMS* music font set are also available for use in text strings.

Plaine and Easie. This melodic input code developed by Barry Brook and Murray Gould in the late 1960's remains important because of its extensive use in thematic indexing projects, especially the manuscript cataloguing effort of the International Inventory of Musical Sources (RISM) coordinated in Frankfurt, Germany. Diverse printing programs for RISM data have been written. Output from one by Norbert Böker-Heil was shown in the *1988 Directory*, p. 19. A program for data verification by Brent Field has been in active use for over the past year. Documentation is available from RISM Zentralredaktion, Sopienstr. 26, W-6000 Frankfurt-am-Main 90, Germany, and John Howard, Music Library, Harvard University, Cambridge, MA 02138; e-mail: *howard@harvarda*.

PLAINSONG. Royal Holloway and Bedford New College (Computer Centre, Egham Hill, Egham, Surrey, UK TW20 0EX, England; e-mail: *C.Harbor@vax.rhbnc.ac.uk*). *PLAINSONG* is a series of programs for transcription, analysis, and printing of music in black square neumatic notation on a four-line stave with C, F, D, or G clefs. It is under development by Catherine Harbor and Andy Reid. *PLAINSONG* runs on the IBM PC. Dot matrix and PostScript laser printers may be used. The work is described in Catherine Harbor, "*PLAINSONG*—A Program for the Study of Chant in Neumatic

Notation," *Computers in Music Research Conference Handbook* (Belfast: The Queen's University, 1991), pp. 24-5.

The Portable Musicwriter. Music Print Corp., 2620 Lafayette Drive, Boulder, CO 80303. This method for printing musical examples, developed by Cecil Effinger, a recognized pioneer in music printing technology, requires an IBM Wheelwriter. The resolution is 104 dpi vertically and 120 dpi horizontally. Music is represented alphanumerically. Slurs are added by hand. Shown in 1990 and previous years.

Professional Composer [p. 56]. Mark of the Unicorn, 222 Third St., Cambridge, MA 02142; tel. (617) 576-2760. This commercial product for the Apple Macintosh has been poorly represented in previous years because of its failure to provide any material other than advertising copy. Its one direct contribution was shown in 1988.

SCORE [pp. 131, 150]. Deriving from an academic research system at Stanford University, Leland Smith's *SCORE* program for IBM PC compatibles is now in use by major music publishers, such as Schott, and many performing organizations. *SCORE* is being used to produce the collected works of J.B. Lully. Optically scanned musical data from the University of Surrey have been converted to *SCORE* data for printing [*cf.* p. 109]. The original input system is alphanumeric and requires separate passes for pitch, rhythm, and articulation. Several supplementary products provide other means of input [*cf. Escort, la mà de guido,* and *ScoreInput*]. Forty music fonts are available. There is a PostScript text font compatibility. The *SCORE* input code was shown in the *1987 Directory*, p. 14.

ScoreInput. Passport Designs, 625 Miramontes Street, Half Moon Bay, CA 94019; tel. (415) 726-0280. *ScoreInput* is a program by Paul Nahay to generate input for Leland Smith's *SCORE* program either from a MIDI keyboard or through redefinition of a QWERTY keyboard. The developer claims that it is faster and more accurate than other front ends for *SCORE*.

SCRIBE. Scribe Software Associates, La Trobe University, Bundoora, Victoria 3083, Australia; tel. +61 03-479-2879. User support is available by fax +61 03-478-5814 and e-mail: *MUSJS@lure.latrobe.edu.au*. This academic research system developed jointly by La Trobe and Melbourne Universities for fourteenth-century music is oriented mainly toward database management of musical repertories. It runs on IBM PC AT-compatibles. It handles entry, display, retrieval, and analysis. Its capability for producing facsimiles of sources with any Hewlett Packard compatible plotter extends to colored notation [shown in grey-scale in the *1988 Directory*, pp. 100-1]. A plotter driver for round notation is under development. Single attributes, such as pitch, may be searched. User-entered data can be merged with pre-packaged data for analytical use. The program is available by license to both individuals and institutional sites and runs in IBM PC compatibles. The original software development was by John Griffiths; Brian Parish is the current software developer. John Stinson is the head musicologist.

Staatliches Institut für Musikforschung. Tiergarten Str. 1, D-1000 Berlin 30, Germany. Music printing programs have been written here for various platforms since the early 1970's by Norbert Böker-Heil. The existing system has been used to produce scores for music publishers. Some special capabilities of the system for contemporary music were shown in the *1988 Directory*, pp. 122-5.

Subtilior Press. 292 Maurice Street, London, Ontario N6H 1C5, Canada; tel. (519) 642-4510. David Palmer's *Subtilior Press* is a program for late-Medieval and Renaissance mensural notation that runs on a Macintosh Plus with *HyperCard*. Transcriptions are assembled on the screen from graphic elements. The price is extremely modest. Examples including illuminated initials, ligatures, and white mensural notation were shown in 1989. CCARH regrets that some early copies of *CM 1990* lacked the developer's name and [now superseded] address.

Synclavier Music Engraving System [pp. 141, 151]. New England Digital Corp., 85 Mechanic St., Lebanon, NH 03766; tel. (603) 448-5870. The Music Engraving System is offered by New England Digital both as a stand-alone workstation and as an adjunct to their larger audio and music processing systems. Information may be entered alphanumerically, via MIDI input, or by on-screen assembly. Some special capabilities, including shape-notes and guitar tablature with MIDI support, are available. PostScript files are produced. Gregg Sewell, an engraver at 518 N. Cherry St., Florence, AL 35630; tel. (205) 764-6212, has engraved examples for recent issues of this publication. Alan Talbot (Graphire Systems, PO Box 838, Wilder, VT 05088) serves as an independent consultant on printing applications of the system and has coordinated all submissions representing this system.

TELETAU. Pisa and Florence, Italy. *TELETAU* is an integrated system for musical data management initially developed at CNUCE in Pisa; it is now maintained jointly with the Florence Conservatory. Details of its encoding system were shown in the *1987 Directory*, p. 22. See commentary on p. 30 (Astra Database) and pp. 105-6.

THEME, The Music Editor. THEME Music Software, PO Box 8204, Charlottesville, VA 22906; tel. (804) 971-5963. This commercial product, developed by Mark Lambert for the IBM PC, has been used extensively in academic settings. Its alphanumeric input system uses a redefined keyboard (shown in 1988). It has a provision for MIDI input and for conversion of alphanumeric files to MIDI output. Optimization of page layout is automatic. Binary-encoded data sets are available to users. Output was last shown in 1989.

TIFF. See *Graphics file formats*.

Toppan Scan-Note System. Toppan International Group, Iwanami Shoten Annex Bldg. 2-3-1, Kanda Jimbocho, Chiyoda-ku, Tokyo 101, Japan. The Toppan system originated in Aarhus, Denmark, where it was developed by Mogens Kjaer. It is at present a proprietary system that accepts electronic keyboard input and prints music with a laser phototypesetter. Toppan Printing Co. Ltd. contracts with major music publishers and has produced some recent volumes of the *Neue Mozart Ausgabe*. Illustrations were shown in 1987.

Wildberger, Melvin [pp. 142, 152]. 113 Alahele Place, Kihei, Maui, HI 96753. Mr. Wildberger, formerly of Nevada City, CA, is a traditional music typesetter who was invited this year to submit examples of his work for the sake of comparison to computer-based settings.

He describes his approach as follows: "The principal advantage of the method of typesetting I practice has been, and remains, the ability to plan a layout *in advance*, taking into consideration musical phrasing, page turns, and economy of reproduction by fitting the material to printers' signatures, which is very often possible. I know of no other system with which the skilled music typesetter can pack more on a page and still maintain good spacing and legibility. In both of these areas computer music typesetting tends to fail miserably. These areas will continue to present severe problems to the music typesetter who tries to use computers to generate layout, because music is not a strictly linear proposition, as are ordinary word typesetting and other applications."

WOLFGANG. Société Mus'Art, Case Postale 26, CH-1242 Satigny, Geneva, Switzerland. This academically oriented music processor, developed by Etienne Darbellay for IBM PC compatibles, became commercially available last year and was awarded the Swiss Prize for Technology for 1990.

The keyboard is fully user-definable. Screen resolutions to 1664 x 1200 are supported. Files can be converted to *TIFF* compressed or uncompressed formats and used with such desktop publishing programs as *Ventura Publisher* and *Aldus Pagemaker*. Dot matrix and LaserJet output is supported. PostScript support is under development, as is an interface for MIDI input. An interface with the ADLIB sound driver exists.

WOLFGANG has the ability to represent and reproduce plainchant, mensural notation (black and white, ligatures), and the unmeasured *style brisé*. It also supports automatic reduction to a two-stave transcription of up to five voices and permits the creation of polylingual scores requiring Arabic, Cyrillic, and Gothic (as well as Roman) characters. Output was shown in 1990.

MIDI Typesetting Services

For those who are reluctant to use music notation programs, MIDI Notes will convert MIDI data submitted on diskette to fully-scored staff notation. This is produced with a laser printer on acid-free paper. MIDI Notes will also provide a title page, a copyright registration, and binding of longer works. Submitted material is carefully checked for musical correctness and is formatted for optimum presentation. The software involved has been developed by Phillip Lui and others. Further information is available from Yee-Ping Wu, MIDI Notes, 55 W. 16th St., Studio 3, New York, NY 10011; tel. (800) 825-MIDI or (212) 807-9608; fax 255-9313.

Index

A Note to Contributors

Computing in Musicology welcomes information on current and recent academic research and software development. Contributors should stress the value of their research to musicologists. Contributors of technical and scientific material should seek to emphasize the value of their work in musical studies. Contributors of historical, theoretical, and analytical applications are encouraged to state how their work is related to other computer-assisted work with similar goals and how their approach could be adapted to other topics. Illustrations that capture the essence of the capability described are highly desirable.

Contributions of more than a few pages should be accompanied by an abstract. Contributions of any length in languages others than English, French, German, or Italian should be accompanied by a résumé in English. It is often helpful to have reference materials in the native language of the author when the submission is in English used as a second language. Almost all material reported in *Computing in Musicology* is significantly condensed. It is therefore to the contributor's advantage to provide succinct information.

Those wishing to be included in the solicitation for contributions of output from notational software programs should contact the Center by March 31. All other contributions must be received by June 30. All contributions should be addressed to *Computing in Musicology*, Center for Computer Assisted Research in the Humanities, 525 Middlefield Road, Suite 120, Menlo Park, CA 94025. Short contributions without illustrations may be sent by electronic mail (*XB.L36@Stanford.Bitnet*) or by fax (415-329-8365); these should be identified clearly as contributions to *Computing in Musicology* and must be accompanied by a complete name, mailing address, and telephone number.

Contributions containing bibliographical citations should be provided when possible both in writing and on a 3.5" or 5.25" diskette readable on an MS DOS machine. Machine-readable submissions should be in generic ASCII or *WordPerfect 5.0* or *5.1*. Only contributions including specially prepared materials (manuals, illustrations, etc.) can be acknowledged.

We thank you for your patience and cooperation.

Computing in Musicology: Style Sheet

Italics: In hardcopy submissions, the following should be italicized: titles of books, journals, and proceedings; titles of major texted musical works, such as operas; and titles of programs and specific versions of computer languages (*e.g.*, *Turbo Pascal*) but not of languages (Pascal) or operating systems (UNIX).

Titles: Titles of articles within books or journals, of short texted musical works, such as songs, and of nicknames for musical works (*e.g.*, "Moonlight" Sonata) should be placed within double quotation marks. For titles in English, the main words should begin with a capital letter. Titles in other languages follow native style.

Names: In bibliographical references, please include first names of authors and editors as well as volume/issue numbers (in Arabic numerals) and page numbers of articles in journals and collected writings. Please observe the name order indicated below.

(1) Single author, book:
> Mazzola, Guerino. *Geometrie der Töne*. Basel: Birkhäuser, 1990.

(2) Single author, article in journal:
> Bel, Bernard. "Time in Musical Structures," *Interface,* 19/2-3 (1990), 107-135.

(3) Single author, article in book or proceedings:
> Morehen, John. "Byrd's Manuscript Motets: A New Perspective" in *Byrd Studies*, ed. Alan Brown and Richard Turbut (Cambridge: Cambridge University Press, 1991), pp. 51-62.

(4) Single author, thesis or dissertation:
> Diener, Glendon R. "Modeling Music Notation: A Three-Dimensional Approach." Ph.D. Thesis, Stanford University, 1991.

(5) Multiple authors, article in journal:
> Hill, John Walter, and Tom Ward. "Two Relational Databases for Finding Text Paraphrases in Musicological Research," *Computers and the Humanities*, 23/4 (1989), 105-111.

Bibliographical listings, which should be limited to eight items, should be given in alphabetical order of the authors' surnames. Multiple references by the same author should be given alphabetically by title.

Citations within the main text may give the author and the year only, *e.g.* "(Hill 1989)". If multiple writings by the same author occur in the same year, please append designations (Hill 1989a, Hill 1989b, etc.) to appropriate bibliographical citations in the reference section.